Alan Harding

22. vi. 2005

THE RECORD SOCIETY OF
LANCASHIRE AND CHESHIRE

FOUNDED TO TRANSCRIBE AND PUBLISH
ORIGINAL DOCUMENTS RELATING TO THE TWO COUNTIES

VOLUME CXL

The Society wishes to acknowledge with gratitude the support given towards
publication by

The Marc Fitch Fund
The Aurelius Foundation
Cheshire County Council
Lancashire County Council

ISBN 0 902593 63 3

Printed in Great Britain by J. W. Arrowsmith Ltd.

*Extenta dominii de Longdendale
anno xxxiiij° Edwardi tercij*

EXTENT OF THE LORDSHIP
OF LONGDENDALE 1360

Edited by John Harrop
with Paul Booth and Sylvia Harrop

PRINTED FOR THE SOCIETY
2005

CONTENTS

ILLUSTRATIONS

Note: Plates 1 and 2 © Mrs Rachel McGuicken, July 2003. Plates 3-14 by John Harrop, all taken in May 2004 except where an earlier date is indicated.

GENERAL EDITOR'S PREFACE

With the publication of this volume, there are grounds for maintaining that the Record Society's 'series' of mid-fourteenth century Cheshire documents has now become established. In 1977, Liverpool University's Paul Booth suggested that the Society publish a succession of parallel Latin/English texts of Cheshire material held by the Public Record Office, accompanied by introductions, notes and other relevant data. In his proposal he observed that modern scholarship could improve considerably on the standard set at the beginning of the twentieth century by the pioneering Cheshire historian Ronald Stewart-Brown, whose *Accounts of the Chamberlain and Other Officers of the County of Chester, 1301–60* was published by the Society in 1910. It is therefore appropriate that this third volume of P.R.O. Cheshire records from the early 1360s is a greatly improved and extended annotated version of material which first appeared in a far less satisfactory form in the *Cheshire Sheaf* between 1976 and 1978. There is also a geographical and administrative overlap in theme between the present volume, dealing as it does with the upland 'panhandle' of Cheshire's easternmost Hundred, and Paul Booth's *Accounts of the Manor and Hundred of Macclesfield, Cheshire, Michaelmas 1361 to Michaelmas 1362*, published as the Society's Volume 138.

The P.R.O. holds over twenty categories of Cheshire records for the fourteenth century. It is hoped that recent volumes may inspire other historians to offer further contributions to the growing picture of later medieval Cheshire life presented by the Society's publications.

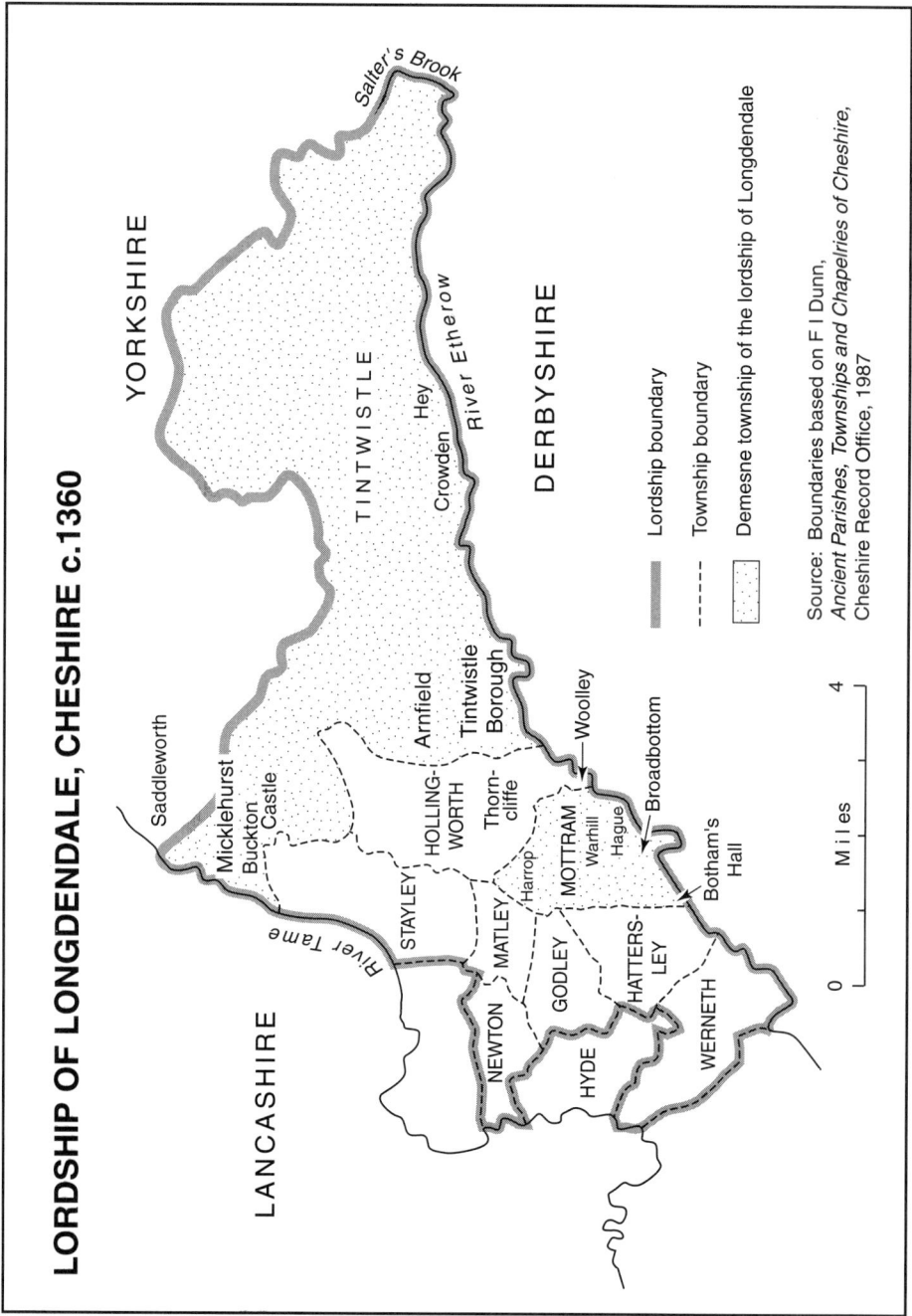

LORDSHIP OF LONGDENDALE, CHESHIRE c.1360

Source: Boundaries based on F I Dunn, *Ancient Parishes, Townships and Chapelries of Cheshire*, Cheshire Record Office, 1987

Lordship boundary
Township boundary
Demesne township of the lordship of Longdendale

Miles 0 4

INTRODUCTION

The 'Extent of Longdendale 1360'

The subject of this study is a roll preserved in the Public Record Office, Kew, in the Special Collections, Rentals and Surveys, Rolls, with the reference SC 11/897. The on-line catalogue (PROCAT) lists it thus:

Longden Dale: Extent or Survey.
34 Edw. III.
Note 7 ms.

The roll bears on the dorse of the last sheet in a later, possibly seventeenth-century, hand: *Extenta dominii de Longdendale anno xxxiiij° Edwardi tercij*, 'Extent of the lordship of Longdendale in the 34th year of Edward the third'. These seven sheets will be described in detail and discussed later, but initially it must be pointed out that none of them constitutes a finished extent or survey of 1360. What survives in this roll amounts to a file of documents of differing types relating to the valuation of the lordship about that time, including two partial and one apparently complete, if defective, rough drafts of an extent of the lordship of Longdendale of 1360, and one later rental and another later extent made for reasons which will be set out below. These surviving records, limited and incomplete as they are, shed interesting light not only on the state of this part of Cheshire at the time, on its people and their vicissitudes and on land tenure, but also on the requirements for and the methodology involved in the preparation of such an extent.

Longdendale

Geographically, Longdendale is the upper portion of the valley of the river Etherow, which in medieval times constituted the boundary between the easternmost portion of Cheshire on its north bank and Derbyshire on its south. It is now often referred to as the Woodhead Valley. Much of the floor of the upper valley is now occupied by a series of reservoirs providing part of Manchester's water supply, the hill tops are grouse moors, and the valley is crossed by the Pennine Way. The modern traveller by road from Manchester to Sheffield may choose to avoid the A59 Snake Pass route and go instead over Woodhead. In so doing he or she will travel up the length of Longdendale, passing through some of the settlements mentioned in these records, and be able to admire the gritstone edges and deep cloughs in the landscape on either side. Since ancient times this was a pack-horse route by which salt from Cheshire was transported to Yorkshire, giving its name to Salter's Brook which provided the boundary with Yorkshire at the eastern end of the valley.

The medieval lordship of Longdendale in the county of Chester occupied not only the north side of the steep valley referred to above, including settlements at Hollingworth, Arnfield and Tintwistle, but most of the so-called 'pan handle' of the old county of Cheshire, including the moorland to the north over into the valley of the river Tame with its castle at Buckton, settlements at Stayley, Micklehurst and Littlehurst (now lost), and lower, broader lands further south-west including settlements at Mottram, Matley, Newton, Godley, Hattersley and Werneth. For maps and plans see map, p. viii, and Nevell and Walker, *Lands and Lordships in Tameside*, pp. 8, 21, 43 and 48.[1]

In addition to the castle at Buckton, already a worthless ruin by the time of this extent, the lordship included two manors in demesne, Tintwistle and Mottram-in-Longdendale. Tintwistle was the lordship's administrative centre and was also a borough. In addition, the lords of the neighbouring townships of Stayley, Newton, Matley, Godley, Great and Little Hollingworth, Hattersley and Werneth held their estates as tenants of the lord of Longdendale, and many of the services which they owed to him are detailed in these records. In view of the publication mentioned above, which discusses (pp. 49–52) the history of the lordship of Longdendale, it may suffice here to provide the following brief explanation of the origins of this record.

The origins of these extents
In the early autumn of 1357 for somewhat complicated reasons the lordship of Longdendale was taken into the hands of the Black Prince in his capacity of earl of Chester.[2] It had been in the possession of Sir Robert Holland, whose father (also called Robert) had been the principal supporter in Lancashire and Cheshire of Earl Thomas of Lancaster.[3] That earl had rebelled against King Edward II, and was defeated and executed at Boroughbridge in 1322. After that battle, Robert Holland, despite his timely desertion of Earl Thomas's cause before the battle, had forfeited all his lands, but he received them back again in 1327. He held Longdendale as tenant of Lancaster's barony of Halton, to which he paid 3s. 4d. a year rent.[4] That barony was held of the earl of Chester by knight service. Between receiving his lands back in 1327 and his death in 1328 Holland passed on Longdendale to his son. The Black Prince's administrators maintained that since this had been done without the earl of Chester's licence, the lordship should be forfeit to the earl as overlord.[5] Such a licence was normally required only if the lands in question were held either by knight service or serjeanty. Although no lord of Longdendale was included in the list of military tenants in Cheshire made in 1288,[6] in membranes 3, 6 and 7 of this record it is stated that several of the lord of Longdendale's tenants held their manors from him by knight service (Stayley, Newton, Matley, Godley, Hattersley, Great and Little Hollingworth, Thorncliffe, Werneth and parts of Mottram), which may perhaps be understood to imply that

1 Michael Nevell and John Walker, *Lands and Lordships in Tameside* (Tameside Metropolitan Borough Council, 1998, hereafter cited as Nevell & Walker).
2 SC 6/802/15, m.1.
3 J.R. Maddicott, *Thomas of Lancaster 1307–22* (Oxford,1970), *passim*.
4 *B.P.R.*, iii. 411–12.
5 *B.P.R.*, iii. 296–7.
6 R. Stewart-Brown, ed., *Calendars of County Court, City Court and Eyre Rolls,* Chetham Society, New Series, 84 (1925), pp. 109-16.

the lordship itself was held by knight service. It is possible that Longdendale was held not of the earl of Chester in chief but as of the manor of Macclesfield, and thus by knight service in this indirect way. The fact that the accounts of the lordship of Longdendale were (as explained below) included amongst those of Macclesfield might be taken to support such a connection.

Longdendale then remained in the Black Prince's hands for seventeen years (1357–74). During that period his officials had to render account for the issues and expenses of the lordship in the same way as they did for his other manors and towns within the county. Nearly all of these Longdendale accounts have survived, most in legible condition, enrolled in random order amongst the various component accounts (such as those of the forest, hundred, borough, parker and stock-keeper) of the manor of Macclesfield, which was geographically contiguous with Longdendale, though separately administered.[7] All these accounts have been used extensively below both to elucidate obscure points in these documents and to add extra information. The accounts indeed provide an understanding of the context in which an extent or rather extents of the lordship were required and clues about some of their dates.

The medieval accounting year normally ran from Michaelmas to Michaelmas (29 September), though for special purposes accounts sometimes covered half a year or periods varying from this norm. In Longdendale most rents normally fell due at one or both of two 'terms', Martinmas (11 November) and Pentecost (i.e. Whit-Sunday, a movable feast varying between 10 May and 13 June) and some other payments were due at the feasts of the Annunciation of the Blessed Virgin Mary, also called Lady Day (25 March), and Michaelmas.

The lands of Robert de Holand in Longdendale were taken into the hands of Thomas le Yonge, escheator of Cheshire, at Michaelmas 1357, and he accounted for them for the period of almost a complete year until 13 September 1358.[8] In the first entry after the title of this account, relating to the rents of freeholders and tenants at will in Tintwistle, Arnfield, Littlehurst and Micklehurst, explicit reference is made to 'the extent made by Delves and the Chamberlain'. The escheator could not present his account without having some such guide as to what his duties required him to account for. That document had evidently been provided by John de Delves, lieutenant-justiciar of Chester, and John de Brunham (alias Burnham) the younger, chamberlain of Chester. Although it is unclear precisely what sources they might have had available to them, it seems likely that it would have been in the form of rentals taken into possession with the lordship.

On 13 September 1358 the prince granted to his devoted friend and companion in arms John Chaundos for the term of his life the stewardship of the lordship of Longdendale and the custody and supervision of his chase there, together with certain other privileges. His deputy Henry de Prestbury submitted the next account for just over half a year from 13 September 1358 to 3 April 1359,[9] encompassing the

7   SC 6/802/15–804/7.
8   SC 6/802/15, m. 1.
9   *Ibid.*

term of Martinmas 1358, but not Pentecost 1359. For this purpose he needed guidance as to what rents and other issues were due at Martinmas term specifically. In this account the first substantial entry again makes reference to 'the extent made by John Delves'.

On 3 April 1359 responsibility for presenting the accounts of the lordship of Longdendale passed to John le Tieu, also described as deputy of John Chaundos and another good servant of the Black Prince, and to whom it may be that some favour was due.[10] His first account runs from 3 April to Michaelmas 1359, including the term of Pentecost only. In the first substantial entry of this account also reference is made to 'the extent made by Delves & Brunham, a transcription of which was delivered on this account.'[11] John le Tieu also presented the next two accounts, the first for the year Michaelmas 1359 to Michaelmas 1360, which again makes explicit reference to 'the extent made by the lieutenant and the chamberlain',[12] and the second for the period from Michaelmas 1360 to 26 March 1361,[13] again including the Martinmas term only. So far as we are aware, no copy of that first extent made by Delves and Brunham, used repeatedly from 1357 to 1360, survives.

It seems likely that it was during John le Tieu's period as deputy steward that the administrative decision was taken to farm out the lordship, that is to let it out at a fixed rent: an arrangement which should have guaranteed the prince's income from the lordship without the associated administrative inconvenience, or the uncertainty which might of necessity arise from fluctuation of population. The lordship accounts for the period from the take-over by the escheator to this time show increasing detail, order and control, particularly in the year Michaelmas 1359 to Michaelmas 1360. It is not clear at what date it was decided that the lessee of the lordship should be Sir William Caryngton, another of the Black Prince's retainers; but it was undoubtedly with a view to clarifying the situation in order to maximise the rent that might be raised from the lordship that it was decided to make a new extent and to take formal evidence for it.

Accordingly the process was begun on 28 January 1360, when a jury which had been summoned from different parts of Longdendale lordship was sworn in and gave its evidence before the officers appointed for the purpose, the same officers who had prepared the extent previously referred to: John de Delves, lieutenant of the Justiciar of Chester, and Master John de Brunham the younger, Chamberlain of Chester. (See the entry numbered **6.01** in the text below.) On an unspecified date, quite possibly the same occasion, another jury from Tintwistle was also sworn in. (See entry **6.08** below.) Those juries and the evidence they provided will be discussed below, but suffice it here to say that documents from two or three stages in the production of this extent from the evidence given by the juries in early 1360 survive amongst the membranes of the roll SC 11/897, but not a complete final version.

10 See Prosopographical Index.
11 SC 6/802/15, m. 1d.
12 SC 6/802/17, m. 5.
13 SC 6/803/3, m. 5.

Doubtless with the aid of that extent a valuation was arrived at, and from Lady Day 1361 the lordship of Longdendale was farmed to Sir William Caryngton for a term of ten years at an annual rent of £40. That might have concluded this phase of extent-making, but it appears that circumstances were on the point of considerable change. Copies of one later Martinmas term rental and one later, much simpler, 'Extent of Longdendale' in rental form survive as membranes 4 and 5 of SC 11/897, both of which show the continuance of many tenancies as they had been before Sir William's time but substantial change in others, as may most readily be seen in the Appendix to this volume. Both these records are datable to between 1361 and 1366, and probably early in that period. After all the trouble and, doubtless, expense involved in the production of the extent of January 1360, something happened which made replacements necessary. A possible explanation appears to be the renewed outbreaks of the Black Death which occurred in 1361 and 1362.[14] The Black Prince's Register in July of 1361 mentions 'this present pestilence'.[15] Presumably it was from these epidemics that sufficient changes in Longdendale tenancies took place, as they evidently did, to render obsolete the extent which had only recently been made.

It might be argued that the £40 per year rent for the lordship in 1361 relied on a very optimistic view of its value, or indeed that it was excessive, even without any deterioration caused by a further loss of population. More than one layer of evidence tends to support such a view. In the first place, in the 1360 extent several of the entries include the words *solet/solebat reddere* 'is/was accustomed to render', suggesting either a situation where the holdings referred to did not bring in the proper amount of rent, usually for lack of tenants (a situation recognised in the accounts) or at least that the tenancy seems to have been uncertain. Secondly, in the Longdendale accounts for the period from the take-over on the prince's behalf at Michaelmas 1357 to March 1361, in no single year had the officials delivered or been expected to deliver such a sum.[16] In the event, however, as is evident from these records, considerable changes did take place in tenancies within the lordship; and as may be seen in the accounts Sir William fell so far into arrears in paying his annual rent that he was deprived of the lordship by the Black Prince's council on 25 March 1366 'for slowness of payment'.[17]

From that date for two years the accounts of the lordship were again submitted by the prince's officials: until 26 March 1367 by Adam de Kyngeslegh, bailiff of the lordship,[18] and for the following year to 25 March 1368 by John de Scolehalgh, steward of the lordship.[19] These officials, like their predecessors,

14 A.R. Myers, *England in the Late Middle Ages*, 8th edition (Harmondsworth, 1971) p. 24.
15 *B.P.R.,* iii. 420.
16 The annual sums required (the appropriate *Et debet* of each account) after all the necessary deductions such as 'decay', allowances, expenses, etc. were: from the Escheator, 1357–58, £33 3s. 2d.; from Prestbury and le Tieu (half a year each taken together), 1358–59, £32 7s. 2d.; from le Tieu, 1359–60, £35 6s. 1d.
17 SC 6/803/12, m. 3.
18 SC 6/803/13, m. 3.
19 SC 6/803/13, m. 4.

required guidance as to their responsibilities, and Kyngeslegh's 1366–67 account makes reference under 'Rents' to 'the rental made by the said Adam in accordance with the demise of the lordship by Sir William Caryngton, late farmer', and against the entry under 'Works' appears a marginal note calling for new extents to be made of ploughing and reaping works. Once again the prince's officials were obliged to put together information on the current state of the finances of the lordship, and were dealing with a situation which had changed considerably from that shown in their previous accounts.

Thus we have external evidence in the Longdendale accounts of an extent made by Delves and Brunham in 1357; internal evidence in this record of another extent also made by Delves and Brunham from the evidence of two juries early in 1360; two separate documents in this record, a rental and another extent, which date from the period 1361–1366; and external evidence in the accounts of a rental made by Adam de Kyngeslegh from information provided by Sir William Caryngton on hand-over in 1366. It is in that context, and against the historical background already described, that the diverse documents which comprise SC 11/897 are to be understood.

The manuscripts

The record preserved in the Public Record Office and now catalogued as SC 11/897 is a roll containing six parchment membranes and one leaf of paper of varying formats and sizes (as indicated below) mounted and sewn together along their top edges between nineteenth-century protective vellum covers. Before the roll reached the Public Record Office it had evidently suffered unsatisfactory storage conditions. It seems likely that the first membrane had at some stage been outermost, having suffered damage from damp and fading that rendered it practically illegible by normal light. Membrane 7 has also suffered serious damage, particularly at the beginning. It is clear that recycled parchment had been used for one of the membranes (m. 3), and another (m. 2) was similarly re-used for a quite unrelated purpose. As indicated above the Roll contains documents of various kinds, some evidently quite rough, their varying formats and contents being outlined below.

Membrane 1, a tall narrow strip of parchment 22.4 cm. high × 6.0–7.7 cm. wide, the front of which was formerly considered illegible, but most of which by the use of ultra-violet light has now been read, bears simply a list of names, of which there were originally 37. On the dorse is the heading *Nomina transgressorum in aqua de Longedendale*, 'Names of trespassers in Longdendale water', which may or may not be connected with the other side. If that is the heading for the list it has a distinct relevance to the purposes of valuation, since if fined only 2d. each they would produce an income of 6s. 2d. It may be significant that from Michaelmas 1359 for one year the fishery of Etherow was farmed out for an annual rent of 6s. 8d. (see entry **6.65** below) and it is possible that this membrane was part of the preparation for that lease. Otherwise it may have been prepared at a later stage when it was again desired to find a farmer for the fishery.

Membrane 2, another tall narrow strip of parchment 29.4 cm. high × 4.0–6.5 cm. wide, presents an untitled summary valuation of the lordship, with an untitled (and unconnected) list of Foresters of Macclesfield two-thirds of the way down the other side which is likely to have been written not before 1362. It is significant that in the Macclesfield accounts for 1359–60, on one membrane between John le Tieu's account for the lordship of Longdendale and a duplicate of the escheator's Longdendale account for 1357–58, is to be found an account of the Foresters and Collectors of Forest-Eyre Fines of the forest of Macclesfield.[20] Clearly, work on these various matters was being conducted by the same personnel in the prince's exchequer, and since parchment was expensive it is perhaps not surprising that this membrane should have been used for different purposes with which the staff were involved, especially if it was for a draft or summary. Clearly a valuation of the lordship was the purpose of the extent. Comparison of the internal evidence with the other membranes and with the Longdendale accounts reveals that this valuation is apparently dependent on m. 6 and the 1359–60 accounts, and may perhaps be dated between Michaelmas 1360 and Lady Day 1361.

Membrane 3, another tall fairly narrow strip of parchment 29.7 cm. high × 9 cm. wide, had previously been used in landscape format for the first line of a charter or similar document written in Anglo-Norman, but was now used in vertical format written on both sides for what was evidently the first sheet of a rough working draft of an extent, in the form of a list of jurors and their statements on oath. The many alterations made to it, some implying verbal and even spelling corrections, indicate that it was probably written during the course of the evidence given by the jurors. After the list of jurors and brief reference to Buckton Castle and a hall, chamber and chapel now leased out, it lists the tenants of the manors of Stayley, Newton, Matley, Godley, and Hattersley, but then has room for only a few of the principal tenants of Mottram. It was apparently the rough draft from which the beginning of the Extent of Longdendale dated 28 January 1360 on m. 6 was copied, of which more will be said below, and was one of possibly several such membranes written in the presence of the jury on that date.

Membranes 4 and 5, neither of which is dated, take a different form and are in a different hand from the others, being set out with mainly one-line entries like rentals, i.e. each entry taking typically the form:

(**4.06**)	*De Henrico Gybon'*	*xviij d.*
i.e.	From (tenant's name) Henry Gybon	rent (in figures) 18d.

Sometimes the tenement also is named, e.g.:

(**5.22**)	*De Rogero de Bothum pro Arnewayfeld*	*xlvj s.*
	From Roger de Bothum for Arnfield	46s.

Sometimes the tenement only is named, perhaps because the previous tenant is no longer in occupation, e.g.:

(**5.16**)	*De burgagio quod fuit Roberti le Smyth senioris*	*vij d.*
	From the burgage which was Robert le Smyth the elder's	7d.

20 SC 6/802/17, m. 5d.

(**5.21**)   *De Ewodeheye*   *xij s.*
      From Ewodeheye   12s.   (Ewodeheye being a field-name.)

Membrane **4**, written on still another tall fairly narrow sheet of parchment 27.5 cm. high × 9.5 cm wide, appears to have been simply copied from a rental, since it contains only rents and individual reveyeld and ward payments (see the section on services below, pp. xxivff.) mainly for the half-year due at Martinmas term (i.e. 11 November). As a rental it does not record payments received in lieu of services. It includes only the rents from Mottram, from Tintwistle with Arnfield, Micklehurst and Littlehurst, and from Hollingworth, omitting rents received from Matley, Godley and Hattersley.

Membrane **5** written on a somewhat broader sheet of paper 29.5 cm. high × 13.5–14.0 cm. wide (an unusual example at such a date of a record of this kind written on paper) is for Martinmas and Pentecost terms, and is headed explicitly *Extenta de Longeden'*, 'Extent of Longdendale'. In addition to rents from Tintwistle and Arnfield, Mottram, Micklehurst and Littlehurst, and of free tenants in Longdendale, it contains monetary values (some defective) for such items as the farm of herbage and agistment, the farm of the mill and stallage, for a number of services provided by the various tenants and also for perquisites of courts. It does not, however, record individual payments of revegeld or ward, providing a lordship total for revegeld only. The text of membranes 4 and 5 continues overleaf in both cases. Their dating will be discussed below.

Membrane 6 is a preliminary draft entitled *Extenta dominij de Longedale* (*sic*), 'Extent of the lordship of Longdendale' dated Tuesday 28 January 1360, written on a sheet of parchment in landscape format 22.5 cm. high × c. 26 cm. wide. Though it contains a vast amount of detail (we have numbered 65 entries), much of it in heavily abbreviated form, there being 29 lines of text on the recto and 33 on the dorse, its contents suggest that it was produced in unusual circumstances. It starts with a properly set-out heading and the list of jurors copied from m. 3, written by the hand which wrote **3.01**, omitting the name of the juror who did not appear. Then in mid-line, for unexplained reasons, the same hand continues the jurors' evidence relating to Mottram, starting where the dorse of m. 3 ends. After the remaining free tenants of Mottram it next lists the tenants of the manors of Great and Little Hollingworth and Thorncliffe. After a gap a second hand, which had written **3.02–18**, writes a second jury's evidence concerning the tenants of 25 burgages and many other tenements in Tintwistle, and the tenants at will of Great and Little Arnfield, of Micklehurst and Littlehurst in the Tame valley, and of various properties in Mottram not previously listed. There follow memoranda relating to necessary service of the mill by the tenants at will of Arnfield, to the tenure by knight service of Werneth by a 15-year-old boy, to the lease of what from the accounts is understood to be the agistment of Longdendale with certain privileges, and to the lease of the fishery of Etherow. All the text on both sides from line 16 was struck through. Like m. 3, this membrane shows many alterations, often indicative of oral input, perhaps best understood as having been written in the presence of the jury.

Membrane 7 is another preparatory draft of part of the (1360) Extent, written on an upright sheet of parchment c. 47 cm. high × c. 24.5 cm. wide, i.e. almost twice the size of m. 6, in a more spacious style, having a ruled left margin and marginal headings for the various sections, with 50 lines of text on the recto and 11 only on the dorse. Although its upper portion is so badly damaged that only small parts of the first six lines and other portions are legible, it is clear that it began with a dated heading and list of jurors apparently copied from m. 6. Then the entries in m. 3 and m. 6 relating to the tenants of manors, townships and other properties held mainly by knight service were copied, with considerable rearrangement into what was presumably the intended order. The sections of m. 6 relating to the borough of Tintwistle and to the tenants at will in Arnfield, the Tame valley and Mottram and two of the closing memoranda are not included in this draft. It is noteworthy, however, that the substance of the first two descriptive entries in m. 6, relating to Mottram, is here found in its proper place following the Mottram entries from the dorse of m. 3, and linking signs were inserted both in the margin of m. 7 and between entries **6.01** and **6.02** for the benefit of the scribe of the next copy. The purpose of this version thus appears to have been threefold: to exemplify the appropriate layout of a final version, to combine the evidence contained in membranes 3 and 6, making important adjustments to the order, and to insert some omitted details of services. It seems likely to date from 1360, perhaps early in the year.

From the foregoing it will be apparent that the membranes of SC 11/897 relate to one another and contribute to the purpose of the valuation of the lordship in varying ways. Apart from m. 1, which has its own character, there is a very great deal of parallelism between the membranes, so that most entries in any one of them may be explained by an entry in one or more others. For example, all the elements included in the summary valuation on m. 2 are to be found mentioned in some form in the other membranes; most of the rents listed in m. 4 and m. 5 are found explained in the statements of m. 3, m. 6 or m. 7; and for most of the statements in m. 3, m. 6 and m. 7 parallel rental entries are to be found in m. 4 and m. 5, though in many cases with different tenants. In these circumstances it is most striking that, apart from the list of jurors at their beginning, m. 3 and m. 6 have totally complementary subject-matter, no other single entry being found in both, even though m. 6 gives the indication that it started by being copied from m. 3. In fact, taken together m. 3 and m. 6 provide full statement evidence for almost all the sums of money regularly referred to in the 1357–60 accounts: see Tables 1 and 2 below. It is this which has led to our understanding outlined above of the development of the 1360 extent, recording the jurors' evidence, from the rough drafts of m. 3 and m. 6 (or possibly a lost membrane or membranes from which m. 6 may have been copied), to the much more accomplished layout and corrected order of m. 7, in preparation for a final version now lost.

The dates of membranes 4 and 5

One of the most problematical concerns in the editing of the documents which comprise this roll has been the question of the dates of membranes 4 and 5 and their status and functions within the corpus. What is clearly apparent from the differences in the details of some of the tenancies listed in these membranes is that they were not made contemporaneously with the January 1360 extent or with each other. Each presents as it were a snapshot of the lordship at the time when it was written; but while some of the characters remain the same from one record to another, others vary. The changes may most readily be seen in the Appendix to this volume, in which are listed side by side the tenancies as recorded in the various membranes.

Until recently it was felt that membranes 4 and 5 had perhaps been written before January 1360, and might relate to the extent(s) referred to in the accounts from 1357 onwards, for after the production of the 1360 extent there should surely have been no need for another such for some time. That understanding did present problems, particularly since in one case at least (that of Dok's family, as illustrated below in the section 'Longdendale at a time of change') it was the younger generation who paid the rents in membranes 4 and 5. By detailed reference, however, to the Longdendale accounts and other source material it will be argued below that both membranes appear to have been written after Lady Day 1361 but before 1366, during Sir William Caryngton's tenure of the lordship, and probably during the earlier part of that period. A cause is therefore required sufficient to explain not only the need to produce these two separate and diverse records comparatively soon after the 1360 extent, but also the changes in tenures which they indicate both from that extent and from one another.

Such a cause is perhaps to be found in the local effects in this corner of Cheshire of the recurring outbreaks of the Black Death which took place in 1361 (mentioned in the Black Prince's Register in July of that year as 'this present pestilence') and 1362.[21] If the epidemic was rampant in the summer immediately after Sir William took over the farm of the lordship, that would provide an explanation both of the need for a new rental at the Martinmas of his first year and of the changes in tenure which it reveals. And if the plague continued or struck again in the following year, that would explain the need after that second outbreak had subsided, presumably not before Pentecost 1362, for another new extent recording the tenancies as they then existed in the changed situation. In the period of up to four years after that new extent was compiled, Sir William fell increasingly into arrears until the lordship was taken back into the prince's hand and Adam de Kyngeslegh became responsible for the 1366–67 account, with its presentation and figures rather different from what had gone before. The detailed evidence for the dates of these two membranes is set out below.

The entries which we have numbered **4.47**, **4.49** and **4.56** all record situations different from those in membranes 3, 6 and 7, and certainly postdate them, as do entries **5.14–15**, **5.31**, **5.33**, **5.35–36** and **5.64**. Entry **5.53** appears to be dependent on and therefore later than the 1359–60 account. As will be shown below, both m. 4 and m. 5 are to be dated between the end of March 1361 and Lady Day

21 *B.P.R.*, iii. 420. Cf. Edward Baines, *History of the County Palatine of Lancaster* (London, 1831), p. 142, and Myers, *England in the Late Middle Ages*, pp. 23f.

1366. Membrane 4 as a Martinmas rental must therefore date to a feast of St Martin within the period 1361 to 1365; but differences from the 1366–67 account mean that it is unlikely to have been made late in that period.

The first highly significant entry for the dating of membrane 4 is **4.68**, which records a payment of 6s. by John de Hyde for land from the wardship of the son of Robert de Holynworth, and relates to payments recorded in the Longdendale accounts for the custody of the lands and tenements (a quarter of Matley) of Henry son and heir of Alice daughter of William de Matley. The same Henry, identified (as more usually) as the son of Robert de Holynworth, was described as tenant of this quarter of Matley in **3.08** (apparently written in January 1360) though the jury on that occasion, which included his father, was not recorded as having mentioned that he was under age and consequently a ward. It is unclear precisely when the Martinmas payment by John de Hyde mentioned in **4.68** was made, though for the following reasons it must have been at or after Martinmas 1361. The first record of a payment of 6s. for that custody (from an unidentified payer) is to be found under 'Rents of assise' in the Michaelmas 1359–Michaelmas 1360 account, in which Henry is described as 14 years of age.[22] That payment was presumably made by or at Michaelmas 1360. Since m. 4 is a Martinmas rental, the payment recorded in **4.68**, which was for a whole year, cannot have been made at Martinmas (11 November) 1360 since that day fell outside the term of the 1359–60 account, and the next account from Michaelmas 1360 to Lady Day 1361, which did include Martinmas 1360, records a half-year's payment of 3s. only. Entry **4.68**, and consequently the whole membrane, must therefore be dated to not before Martinmas 1361.

A second possibly significant matter is found in entries **4.50–52** and **4.54**, which reveal increased rents from the tenants of Micklehurst and Littlehurst intermediate in amount between the rent mentioned in **5.38** (identical with that of **6.47**) and those in the 1366–68 accounts. If that intermediate rent was due at an intermediate time, m. 4 would need to be dated later than m. 5, which is difficult to reconcile with the overall impression given by both membranes. (See Appendix, p. 80.) If, as will be argued below, m. 4 came first, then these rents had first been increased by Sir William to this level presumably on take-over, then in m. 5 they were restored to what they had been previously, then in due course by 1366 they were increased again even more. (See Appendix, p. 80 and Table 3, p. xl.) If that was the series of events, m. 4 could date from as early as Martinmas 1361, and this new rental would have been necessitated by the changes in tenancy which had taken place since the extent of January 1360, probably resulting from the pestilence active in 1361. Membrane 4, therefore, appears to be dated not before Martinmas 1361, but possibly of that year.

Adam de Kyngeslegh's 1366–67 account refers to a rental he made on evidence provided by Sir William Caryngton in 1366, but the situation revealed in that account had changed considerably from the one apparent in this membrane. This

22 SC 6/802/17, m. 5.

m. 4 rental cannot have been the one which Adam de Kyngeslegh himself made, but may have been part of the material handed over to him by Sir William in 1366 on which his rental was based.

In membrane 5, entry **5.17** recording a rent of 7d. from Simon the smith's forge must postdate not only entry **6.31** but also the accounts from Michaelmas 1359 to 26 March 1361,[23] in all of which that property was 'in decay', that is had no tenant and produced no rent; and entry **5.25** recording the receipt of 12d. for a property called *herstancloghous'* which similarly was 'in decay' in **6.21** and in all the accounts from 1357 to 26 March 1361 must also postdate all those accounts. These two entries thus place this document also after the beginning of Sir William de Caryngton's farm of the lordship.

On the other hand, in 1364 Sir John de Hyde sold to Richard de Mascy of Sale a number of properties including a messuage and 14 acres of land in Stockport, Mottram-in-Longdendale and Baggelegh.[24] If that sale included the land in Mottram for which Sir John de Hyde paid 13d. rent in entry **5.50**, that is the one messuage and seven acres which he held in Mottram by knight service as described in entry **3.15**, that would provide a not inappropriate *terminus ante quem* for this membrane, but that inclusion remains to be confirmed.

Another entry significant for the dating of m. 5 is **5.36**, which records under Mottram 'From Adam le Tayllour 10s. 1d. in decay'. This Adam is not named anywhere else in the membranes of SC 11/897, and it is altogether unclear from which lands this considerable rent may have been due. (See footnote 158, pp. 37ff. and Appendix, p. 81.) In these circumstances it appears that Adam's tenancy had been entered into after the Martinmas to which m. 4 relates, but was now in decay, suggesting at least some lapse of time between the two membranes. The developments concerning the tenancies of Dok's family, quoted and discussed below in the section 'Longdendale at a time of change', also reveal what seems to be a natural progression from m. 6 through m. 4 to m. 5. Membrane 5 ought thus to be dated not only after Sir William de Caryngton's take-over of the farm of the lordship of Longdendale at Lady Day 1361, but also subsequent to the Martinmas of m. 4.

Although most figures in this membrane do not correspond with the 1366–68 accounts, one may be seen to tend in that direction. The £7 11s. 8d. total from Tintwistle and Arnfield at **5.27** appears again in those accounts as the rent of Tintwistle 'termors', and may have continued from this record until then. Membrane 5 correlates also with the valuation in m. 2 in two significant details. The figure of 13s. 1d. for the works due from Stayley appears in both **2.04** and **5.53**, and may derive from the 'Respites' section of the 1359–60 accounts where that figure is first mentioned. On the other hand, the value of £4 for the farm of the mill and stallage in the somewhat defective entry **5.41** is also to be found in **2.11**, but is supported by none of the accounts. In 1360 it might have been prompted by optimism, but circumstances were to render it totally unrealistic: see

23 SC 6/802/17, m. 5; 6/803/3, m. 5.
24 Earwaker, ii. 157.

the relevant 1366–68 figures given in Table 3, p. xl. The presence of that figure of £4 in m. 5 may be interpreted as tending to support a date for this membrane fairly early in Sir William's tenure.

A. R. Myers states that the Black Death revived in both 1361 and 1362,[25] and the changes from m. 4 evident in m. 5 (see Appendix, pp. 72ff.) may be understood to imply that loss of life from epidemic had not ceased by the Martinmas represented by m. 4. By Pentecost 1362, or perhaps more likely at a date somewhat later, the plague subsided and it became appropriate to make a replacement not only for the January 1360 extent but also for the Martinmas rental. This m. 5 extent, set out in simple rental style for Martinmas and Pentecost terms, appears to have been what was produced for that purpose. Like m. 4, this membrane also may have been included in the material handed over to Adam de Kyngeslegh in 1366 at the suspension of Sir William's farm of the lordship.

We are thus left with the conclusions that both m. 4 and m. 5 were made during the period 1361–1366, m. 4 perhaps at Martinmas 1361 and m. 5 possibly by 1364, perhaps as early as 1362, and that the differences found in them not only from the extent made in January 1360, but also from each other, are likely to have arisen at least in part as results of the pestilence of 1361–62. The consequent changes in tenure had rendered obsolete the deliberately-compiled 1360 extent, and the management of the lordship had required the production of not one but two successive new records to replace it.

The juries of the 1360 extent and their evidence

The jury which met on 28 January 1360 (see entry **3.01** below) consisted of twelve principal tenants of the lordship, the men who held the manors of Stayley, Newton, Great and Little Arnfield and one third of Little Hollingworth, the representative (perhaps son) of the tenant of two-thirds of the manor of Little Hollingworth and Thorncliffe, the father of the fourteen-year-old tenant of a quarter of the township of Matley, and the tenants or their representatives of Dewsnap and another property in Mottram, and Wallcroft in Tintwistle, a leading farmer of the agistment of Longdendale, and two of the five joint tenants of Micklehurst and Littlehurst in the Tame Valley. The tenant of Broadbottom in Mottram, who also had been included in the first list, did not appear. On an unspecified but quite possibly the same date another jury, only four of whose names are listed (see entry **6.08** below), was also sworn in: those named (three of whom were also members of the first jury) were holders of burgages and other lands in Tintwistle. This may perhaps have been or represented the jury of a borough court of Tintwistle.

These juries gave on oath statements about who held each property in the lordship and on what conditions, that is whether *per servicium militare*, 'by knight service', *in feodo*, 'in fee' (by hereditary right) or *ad voluntatem*, 'at will' (at the lord's will) and by what rents and services. One manor, Arnfield (see the entry **3.05** below), is described by the expression *quod dimittitur ad firmam*, 'which is leased at a fixed rent'. On the first rough draft (m. 3), after their names are list-

25 Myers, *England in the Late Middle Ages,* p. 24.

ed, all but one with the abbreviated form *Jur'* alongside to indicate that they were present and had been sworn in, and the introductory formula *qui dicunt super sacramentum suum quod ...*, 'who say upon their oath that...', their statements appear to be arranged more or less hierarchically, beginning with Buckton Castle and a 'hall chamber and chapel' now leased out, which may perhaps be understood as the (possibly former) principal manor, then go fairly systematically round the different parts of the lordship, beginning with tenants by knight service of various manors. As indicated above, these statements were recorded in the first place in very rough form on a small scrap of re-used parchment, in this roll now membrane 3, followed probably on the enigmatically arranged membrane 6 (or possibly on one or more lost membranes from which it may have been copied). The modern reader with an interest in either the history of Longdendale and Tameside or local genealogy or indeed in life more generally in this part of England in the middle ages is fortunate that these statements survive *in extenso*, containing as they do some very illuminating information not only on land-tenure, but also on the inhabitants and their way of life.

Succeeding stages in the production of the 1360 extent

The evidence of these juries now needed to be brought into order. As has been described, membrane 3 is in very rough, almost *ad hoc*, form on re-used parchment. Membrane 6, though written on a larger parchment membrane, and beginning with the necessary formal heading and date according to the usual pattern for such records, followed by the list of jury apparently copied from m. 3, then rather surprisingly continues with the remainder of the text, apparently following on from the end of m 3d. The contents of the two membranes together appear to cover the whole of the lordship. Both show much evidence of corrections of a kind associated with verbal communication, as well as others which may arise in normal transcription or editing. From this material the intended extent now needed to be organised. How long and complex such a task normally was we do not know, but in the case of this extent a further draft clearly intended as preliminary or intermediate survives in membrane 7.

It might be reasonable to assume that it was fairly quickly that the same clerks began the required rearrangement. This draft (m. 7) was evidently copied from m. 3 and part of m. 6, arranging the material in a different, more systematic and presumably the intended order as follows. The heading including the list of jurors (**6.01**) was copied from m. 6, then from m. 3 the entries concerning Buckton Castle, the principal manor and the tenants of the manors or townships of Newton, Matley, Godley, Hattersley and Mottram (**3.02** to **3.18**) reserving Stayley (**3.04**) and rearranging **3.18**. Then the remaining entries concerning Mottram (**6.02–03**) were copied from m. 6 in their proper order. Next was inserted the entry on Werneth, which had been slipped into m. 6 almost as an afterthought as a memorandum at **6.62**, followed on the dorse of m. 7 by the entries concerning Hollingworth (**6.04–07**) and Stayley from **3.04**. Though more formally set out as described above, with marginal headings on a still larger parchment membrane, it shows clear evidence, to which attention is drawn in the footnotes to the translation, of having been intended as a preparatory document to guide the scribe of the next copy. All its text, like most of that of m. 6, has been struck through.

The administrators' concern with possibly profitable detail may be seen in the cumulative insertions from one draft to the next. Many entries on m. 6d. have an interlineated addition concerning the payment of various sums of pence for 'reveyeld' and 'ward' (see the section on services below). In m. 7 will be noted in particular the addition of the service *facit sectam ad molendinum domini*, 'he/she makes suit to the lord's mill', i.e. the obligation on tenants to take their grain to the lord's mill for milling, which is here stated as required of several Mottram and Hollingworth tenants but had not been mentioned in m. 3 or m. 6. It is also likely that it was concern over services and their monetary value which caused the entry on the manor of Stayley to be moved in m. 7 from the beginning of the list to the end. Robert de Stavelegh had at the meeting of the jury (**3.04**) been given notice to show by what services (in addition to knight service) he held the manor. From the Longdendale account for 1359–60[26] we learn that Robert de Stavelegh, in arguing that he did not owe the works and services, had shown written evidence of a relaxation by his previous lord, Robert Holand, of the sum due for rent, works and services. When m. 7d. was written the same entry from m. 3 was copied out (**7.27**), but was later struck through, suggesting that the evidence provided for the account may perhaps have sufficed, at least temporarily, for both purposes.[27]

Our assumption has been that though we have so far found no trace of it the intended final full and correct version of the 1360 extent was in due course completed from these drafts. The striking through of the texts of most of m. 6 and all of m. 7 may perhaps be taken to imply that their copying had been completed. In the Longdendale accounts referred to above, one year of which (1361–62) edited by Paul Booth has been published in the Record Society's previous Volume 138,[28] there are frequent references *sicut continetur in (eadem) extenta*, 'just as is contained in the (same) extent', which appear to refer to a record which might serve as authoritative.

The remainder of Sir William Caryngton's tenure of the lordship
The lordship was returned to Sir William for life on rather different conditions, the details of which need not concern us here, on 11 April 1368.[29] Yet Sir William's tenure of the lordship came to an end on 28 November 1374, when it was returned to the Holland family in the person of Maud Holland and her husband John, Lord Lovel of Titchmarsh.[30] Additional evidence relating to the lordship during Sir

26 SC 6/802/17, m. 5.
27 The dispute, however, appears to have rumbled on, appearing as a 'respite' in the accounts for 1360–61, 1367–75, SC 6/803/3, m. 5 – 804/7, m. 3d.
28 P.H.W. Booth, ed., *Accounts of the Manor and Hundred of Macclesfield … 1361–62*, R.S.L.C., cxxxviii, hereafter cited as *Maccl. Acc.*
29 SC 6/803/15, m. 2d.
30 SC 6/804/7, m. 3d.

William's tenancy may be seen in certain *County Court of Chester Indictments Roll* entries for 1373[31] which record presentments against Sir William not only for hunting, but for widespread demolition of buildings and the felling and disposal of timber during his tenure. This was an indictment only, not the outcome of the case, but it is difficult to envisage such presentments being made while the buildings mentioned were still standing, and we may perhaps be justified in understanding the events underlying the indictment as the asset-stripping of the lordship on his part, possibly occasioned by his recognition of its inability to provide sufficient regular income to pay the rent.

Services

In addition to knight service, by which the various manors and other principal holdings of the lordship were held, these membranes, especially m. 3, m. 6 and m. 7, are very particular in describing some of the services by which tenants held their lands. In the order in which they appear, the first detailed description is to be found in the entry **3.05**:

> 'Item, Robert de Neuton holds the manor of Newton by knight service and by the services of finding for every termor tenant of his one man for 3 days at harvest time at one meal per day, that is to say bread, butter and milk, at the manor of Arnfield which is let at fixed rent, and in Lent for every aforesaid tenant one plough for three days at one meal per day, that is to say for one plough 6 oat cakes, 6 herrings and one gallon of ale, and the lord will find for them forage and a house for the plough animals at the costs of the said tenants.'

That, at least, is the description, and presumably reflects long-standing tradition. **3.12–13** indicate that the tenants of Hattersley were liable to similar ploughing and reaping services.

Entry **3.06** introduces another not uncommon service in rather cryptic form. Above the statement that W. de Hyde held half of the manor of Matley there appears interlineated the expression *drive & lede*. This entry is paralleled in entry **7.04**, but the membrane is illegible at that point and sheds no further light on this expression. On another membrane, however, in entry **6.06** we are told *inter alia* that Christiana de Holyn', who holds two-thirds of Little Hollingworth and Thorncliffe, will amongst her other services also *drive & lede*, and this time the parallel **7.25** is more help, since in place of that vernacular expression it has *et facit sectam ad molendinum domini*, 'and she makes suit to the lord's mill', making it clear that she was expected to 'drive' her corn to and 'lead' her meal from that mill situated at Tintwistle. That obligation on tenants, even from a fairly distant manor such as Matley, could be extremely valuable not only to the miller, but also to his lord.

A second full description of a service is to be found among several mentioned in entry **3.08**:

31 See CCCIR 1373 in Abbreviations below, p. xxxvii.

'Item that Henry son of Robert de Holynworth holds another quarter of the same manor (i.e. Matley) by the same service (i.e. knight service) and by the service of 4s. for the whole manor, and by haghehag, that is finding 6 men for 1 day without a meal in order to make a hay for the lord's venison each year, and by the service of making earthwork at Tintwistle mill whenever it shall be necessary, and of making suit at Mottram Court, and of finding two doomsmen.'

After knight service and rent that entry introduces several interesting new elements: first the delightfully-named 'haghehag' (various spellings of this presumably local English word appear) which we could not possibly understand, as also presumably the Prince's officials could not, were it not so specifically defined in connection with the maintenance of the deer-hay which played an essential part in the regular annual management of the beasts in the prince's chase; next the provision of earthwork, presumably for the leat or perhaps also dam, at Tintwistle mill whenever necessary, i.e. not only for storm damage, but presumably also for regular maintenance; then the very widespread obligation of suit of court, i.e. the obligation to attend regularly; and finally the provision of doomsmen for the court, whose duty was to 'deem the dooms', i.e. preserve in oral tradition and pronounce on the customs of the manor, and sometimes to determine new ones. It will be seen in other entries that many of these services were owed by other tenants also.

What is clear not only from entries **5.54–56** below but also from the Longdendale accounts from 1357–58 onwards is that the ploughing and reaping services due from Newton with their very interesting dietary provisions, and the other customary services of various kinds due from Stayley and Hattersley, including haghehag, were regularly commuted for cash payments which give the appearance of being already customary. So much so indeed that in 1359–60 (the year before he was granted the lease of the lordship) an allowance of rent of 6d. for Haghagh was made because Sir William Caryngton refused to pay the rent but wanted to do the custom.[32] It was not until Sir William's own account for the year 1361–62, however, that a monetary value of 12d. was placed on the works of the mill due from Matley, a figure which may be included in **2.05**.

It is in **3.13** that we encounter also the first mention of two other rather more problematical services:

And the same Richard (de Eton) and William (de Caryngton) render to the lord for reveyeld and ward 9d.

All the entries in these manuscripts relating to these two words refer to cash payment. In this case neither 'reveyeld' (or 'revegald') nor 'ward' is defined in this

32 SC 6/802/17, m. 5. In the light of the allegations of unlawful hunting to be made against Sir William in 1373 (see CCCIR 1373 in Abbreviations below, p. xxxvii) it is difficult to know whether this stand taken by him arose from a belief that the annual rent was being paid for a service which in reality took place more rarely, or from a desire to become more closely acquainted with the management of the deer in the chase.

record, and we are obliged to look elsewhere for assistance. Both words are clearly vernacular.

From its etymological elements, *Reveyeld* must imply a tax paid to or for a reeve of some kind, whether of high rank in a shire or town or more local. In the Longdendale accounts from 1357 onwards[32*] 10s. reveyeld yearly is regularly accounted for under the heading 'Expenses' and described as *comp' in resoluc' redd' dno de Macclesfeld*, 'accounted for in the repayment rendered (*or* of rent) to the lord of Macclesfield.' The payment was also received from other parts of Macclesfield manor. Paul Booth considers[33] that reveyeld was probably 'an ancient communal due paid towards the wages of the earl's aboriginal official, or reeve, of the manor-Hundred.'

The first definition of *Ward* offered by the *O.E.D.* is 'Action of watching or guarding. The action or function of a watchman, sentinel, or the like; look-out, watch, guard.' This service therefore seems likely to have been a money payment in lieu of ward service, i.e. guard duty at a castle. The Longdendale accounts for 1366–67[34] record that by a decision of the prince's council a sum of 3s. 4d. was to be paid out of those accounts to the lord of Halton because that had been paid of old. It seems at least possible that this payment was for Ward, in which case the service so commuted would presumably have been performed at Halton castle.

Another unusual kind of service, or perhaps it would be better described as a rent in kind, appears in entry **6.03**:

> Item, William de Caryngton holds one place called Harop in the same township (Mottram) by knight service and renders yearly 18d. and 1 lb. of cumin.

Evidently this exotic import from the Mediterranean region had been a traditional part of the rent for this particular plot of ground.

As indicated above, these works and services had customarily been commuted for cash payments, which formed an important element in the value of the lordship, so much so that they were regularly listed next after rents in the Longdendale accounts. (See Table 1.) In the 1359–60 accounts are to be found not only the regular sums of 11s. 1d. from Newton for the ploughing and reaping services quoted above, 9s. 9d. for works from Stayley, 3s. 6d. from Hattersley, 10s. from tenants of the lordship for a custom called Reveyeld, and 3s. 3½d. from the same tenants for another custom called Ward, but also rather particularly '4s. from the price of 24 works at Haghag, 2d. per work, of which in Matley 6 works, in Godley 6 works, in Hattersley 2 works, in Hollingworth 9 works.[35] Further, during the suspension of Sir William Caryngton's farm of the lordship, in the margin of the bailiff's account of March 1366–March 1367 there

32* SC 6/802/15, m. 1, etc.
33 See now *Maccl. Acc.*, p. xvii.
34 SC 6/803/13, m. 3.
35 SC 6/802/17, m. 5 and 6/803/1, m. 6. Cf. also *Maccl. Acc.*, pp. 26–7, when the scribes of both surviving versions made clerical errors. The arithmetical discrepancy both here and there arose because there ought to be 3 works in Hattersley. See entries **3.12**, **5.57** and **7.12** below. **3.13** and **7.13** no longer applied since Sir William Caryngton had elected to do the custom instead. See above, p. xxv.

appears the note: *Let new extents be made for these ploughing & reaping works.*[36] It is unclear whether this would have involved a revaluation of them.

Evidence relating to everyday life and economy

For most inhabitants of the lordship in the 1360s life was naturally dominated in the first place by the cycle of agriculture, with the 'ploughing in Lenten time' and 'reaping in harvest time' mentioned amongst the services above, which would of course be carried out on their own or their land-holder's behalf as well as in service to the lord, together with all the other normal agricultural and horticultural activities. The accounts reveal more clearly what is not expressly stated in entry **6.63**, that the 'herbage, focage and arable' of Longdendale were leased out for an annual rent of £12 to a consortium of tenants who are not named there, but of whom William Geffrou was a principal. Entry **6.64** lists the privileges included in this lease: 'And they shall have the *becage* (payment for pasturage of cattle) of the bushes (or scrub-land) of Holyn reasonably with pannage, pasture and tolls, and with fines for straying animals through the whole of Longedendale.'

Secondly, the 1358–59 Longdendale account states that on 13 September 1358 the Black Prince granted to John Chaundos not only the stewardship of the lordship of Longdendale, but also 'the custody and supervision of his chase there'. Within these records that chase explicitly produced the annual requirements of the service of 'haghehag' discussed above, which was likely to have been required at the Hague in Mottram, and certainly by 1370 *extransversum le Crowdenes*, 'out beyond Crowden', where there was evidently another deer-hay. Nothing further is said explicitly of the chase in these records, and it is unclear what effect the change of ownership might have had upon its management. Although royal forests were governed by very strict laws, the principal purpose of which was the preservation of the beasts of the forest, and in particular the red and fallow deer, it is unclear precisely what laws were applicable within this chase, which continued to be private despite having been escheated to the prince. Yet the residents of much of the lordship of Longdendale are likely to have lived their lives within an environment in which in very many ways those beasts had priority. That is the reason why the interestingly-named *becage*, the fee for pasturing cattle in a forest, was due from those who did so in the 'shrag' of Hollingworth. See entry **6.64** below, with note 260 *ad loc.*

The Cheshire side of the river Etherow in Longdendale from the unidentified *Rontandebrok* to Salter's Brook was managed as a fishery, which in 1359–60 was leased to Peter de Ardern for 6s. 8d. Membrane 1 may be a list of trespassers in this fishery at some unspecified date. The accounts reveal that in a number of years there was difficulty in finding a tenant willing to take on the lease.

The lord's mill at Tintwistle milled the grain for the populations not only of Mottram and Tintwistle, but also of Hollingworth, Matley and Hattersley, and their use of its service was in many cases required as a condition of their tenure, expressed either in Latin as *faciunt sectam ad molendinum domini*, 'they

---

36 SC 6/803/13, m. 3.

make suit to the lord's mill' or by the more elliptical vernacular 'drive and lead'. Godley is not mentioned in this connection, but in entry **7.03** there is a reference relating to Newton which is most unfortunately damaged, leaving the situation of its inhabitants in this respect unclear. The maintenance of the mill at Tintwistle required manpower for earthwork, provided whenever required as mentioned above under 'Services'. At this time the mill was operated by William le Mulner.

There may also have been a mill in the valley of the Tame or one of its tributaries, since one of the joint tenants of Micklehurst and Littlehurst was Simon le Muleward (*molendinario* in **4.54**). Another miller, Christian name defective, is amongst the names listed on m. 1: le mulnere de Cyntyll.

Entry **3.05** with its very precise requirements relating to the provision of ploughing and reaping services by the lord of Newton and his tenants, quoted above under 'Services', provides an interesting glimpse of the diet which working people might enjoy; each reaping man's meal in harvest time consisting of 'bread butter and milk', and in Lenten time for each plough team (presumably a man and a boy) one meal consisting of '6 oat cakes, 6 herrings and one gallon of ale'. Since in 1360 and for some years previously the services themselves had customarily been commuted for cash payment, these requirements presumably represented long tradition, but there seems to be no reason to suppose that the diet had changed. Clearly these requirements presuppose local baking, especially of oatcakes, and brewing of ale, and the supply of salt herrings in Lent.

These records also provide some evidence of trade, industry and other occupations. One local industry is indicated only by the occupational surname of Thomas le Barker, who was presumably involved in the preparation of bark for tanning. In addition to a burgage, he held in partnership with John Hobberode a plot of land for which they paid 10s. a year, and which might well have sufficed for a tannery, though it is not named as such. The wife of Tho. le barker paid 4s. 6¾d. rent as a tenant at will in Tintwistle in the 1408 Rental.

A trade mentioned only in a single occupational surname is that of Adam le Tayllour, whose rent of 10s. 1d., under Mottram, was 'in decay' in **5.36**. Since he is not mentioned elsewhere it has not been possible to identify further either himself or his presumably extensive land(s).

Other trades or occupations, not all necessarily practised within the lordship, are expressed or hinted at in the names Adam le Botelir (Butler); John son of Thomas le Forster (Forester); Thomas le Foucher (probably a butcher of venison); Robert le Merser (dealer); Thomas le Spener (?); William le Stiwardesson; and perhaps also the defective Henry le Tern[..].

By far the most intriguing and tantalising industrial reference, however, is to be found in the deleted Tintwistle entry **6.26b** at the beginning of the third line of m. 6d.: *Item* [[*the same Mag'* (Magot Dok's wife) *holds le Smolterhouses which were John son of William de Hyde's and renders yearly 12d.*]] The section indicated by the double square brackets was struck through, with the explanation *because below* inserted above the line. Though deleted, this entry is highly significant. It indicates quite clearly that Magot Dok's wife in fact occupied these premises and paid the rent, but it needed to be, and was, accounted for in a different entry, presumably the one below relating to John son of William de Hyde. And the very name *le Smolterhouses*, which appears nowhere else in these records, provides documentary evidence from 1360 of the metal-smelting industry in Tintwistle. Both Dr Michael Nevell of the Field Archaeology Unit at Manchester University and Dr John Barnet, Senior Survey Archaeologist, Peak District National Park Authority, inform us (private communications) that although lead must be a possibility, iron is perhaps more likely to have been the metal involved, using what is called 'bog-iron', which occurs in this kind of landscape. The form of the word itself is interesting. When this difficult deleted entry was first read by ultra-violet light the word was seen as *Smelterhouses*, but on further examination it was considered that the first vowel is *o* rather than *e*. This may represent a local variant pronunciation, or perhaps an early form of the word, since this is the earliest example of its use so far recorded. (The word 'smolt' in either of its senses 'young salmon' or 'lard' appears most unlikely to be what was involved in this context.) Although metal-smelting has been conducted in these islands since Roman times and must throughout have been spoken of in the vernacular, the earliest citation given in the second edition of *O.E.D.* for 'smelt' in this sense is of 1543, and for 'smelter' of 1455 (both involving lead and both at Fountains Abbey).

It may be that the existence of this industry in Tintwistle helps to explain the number of smiths named in these membranes. In entry **6.28** Henry le Smyth of Stokport is described as holding in fee one messuage with a certain forge for which he renders 6d. a year, and this is likely to be the property for which the Martinmas rent of 3d. is recorded as received from Thomas the Smith in **4.40**. Entry **6.30** lists one messuage upon or above *le Syk*, which was Robert le Smyth the elder's, rendering 7d. a year. This was still occupied by an unnamed tenant at the same rent in **5.16**. Entry **6.31** describes Symon le Smith's plot with curtilage as lying in decay but formerly rendering 9d. a year, and indeed the burgage was recorded under 'Decay of Rent' in the Longdendale accounts from Michaelmas 1359 to Lady Day 1361, but **5.17** records the later annual receipt of 7d. from it. In entry **5.15** one Robert le Smyth, named only here in these manuscripts and presumably a new tenant, pays an annual rent of 12d. for a burgage in Tintwistle, which may have been one of those which had been 'in decay' in m. 6. No other occupation provides so many individuals named in these records.

It is known from the accounts that there were two courts in the lordship, one at Mottram, which from the accounts seems to have conducted more business, or at least received more 'perquisites', and one at Tintwistle, which may have been a borough court. In these records it is only the Mottram court which is explicitly mentioned, and that in connection with the obligations towards it of those who held various manors. The tenants of a quarter of the manor of Matley, the manor of Great Hollingworth and a third of the manor of Little Hollingworth were obliged to perform suit, that is put in an appearance, at Mottram court, which entry **6.04** indicates took place every three weeks; and doomsmen, whose role has been described above in the section on 'Services', were to be supplied for the court, two by the tenant of a quarter of the manor of Matley, three by the tenants of the manor of Great Hollingworth and one third of the manor of Little Hollingworth, and one each by the tenants of the manors of Stayley and Hattersley. Although the court at Tintwistle is not mentioned in these membranes, it is possible that the jurors who gave the evidence relating to Tintwistle in m. 6 were members of the jury of that court.

Comparison with the accounts

At this point it is helpful to consider what may be learned from careful comparison between most of the membranes of the extent and the accounts for the periods when the lordship was taken into the Black Prince's hands. In order to facilitate such comparison the significant figures from each have been presented in tabular form (Tables 1, 2 and 3). In Table 1 the figures are taken from the first part of each account, where the escheator, deputy steward or bailiff listed what he was answering for. It was for this purpose that an extent was required, and all the accounts in Table 1 make specific reference to an extent, a circumstance which lends force to these comparisons. For economy of space and clarity the Roman numerals such as *xij li. xij s. v d.* have been presented in modern form as *£12 12s. 5d.* In the third account in Table 1 will be found the surprising figure of 9⅝d. Such figures are liable to appear where the original makes reference to half a farthing: in this case the fractions of a penny were *ob. di. qu.*, that is a halfpenny and half a farthing. It will be seen that the figures listed here (like others) do contain an occasional arithmetical error, for example in the sub-total under Works in the second and fifth accounts, and one cannot but wonder whether the £7 6s. 2½d. in the top line of the second account (Prestbury's) may not contain a scribal error (*vij li.* for *vj li.*) Inconsistent figures have been printed shaded. It will be noted that throughout the period 1357–60 the works due from Stayley are given as 9s. 9d.; that the mill and stallage were farmed at £3 yearly, the accounts indicating in several cases that the farm had been 'by the steward', and that the farm of the fishery first appears in John le Tieu's 1359–60 account. As explained in the accompanying note, the figure for 'Increase of Rent' in the fourth account includes such items as land newly occupied and three different consequences of the murder of Geoffrey de Honford. These are items which would not necessarily be readily apparent in an extent.

In Table 2 the figures have been partly extracted and partly compiled from each membrane as follows. In m. 2 it was necessary to subtract the interlineated figures which represent reveyeld and ward from the main sums on the lines where that applies. For purposes of reasonable comparison m. 4 has needed rather more interpretation, since in that membrane individual payments of revegeld are listed and therefore needed to be subtracted from the totals to provide the totals for rents. Also, down to the entry **4.63** the membrane presents regular Martinmas term half-yearly figures for Mottram, Tintwistle (including Arnfield, Micklehurst and Littlehurst) and Hollingworth, but in **4.64–68** presents whole year figures for Matley and apparently also for the wardship of Robert de Holynworth's son, then in **4.69–72** reverts to half-yearly rents and reveyeld from Tintwistle and

Hollingworth. The arithmetic therefore in most cases is ours. In the m. 5 table the Tintwistle and Mottram rents have needed to be adjusted by the inclusion of those appearing lower down the membrane from Micklehurst and Littlehurst and from Mottram free tenants respectively using the clerk's own totals. This membrane does contain a number of arithmetical errors. For the mm. 3/6 table the figures have been compiled from the jurors' statements. It will be noticed that no monetary value is there given to the various ploughing and reaping works described as due from Newton, Stayley or Hattersley, or to the 'haghehag' due from several manors, though those values do appear in membranes 2 and 5.

In Table 3 as in Table 1 the figures have been taken from the first part of each account. In both years considerable changes are to be seen from the situation revealed in Table 1, especially under 'Rents', 'Issues of the Mill, Stallage, Fairs & Fishery' and 'Agistment'.

Comparison of the three tables with one another, and comparison of the various membranes of SC 11/897 with one another and with the accounts, has allowed the conclusions to be drawn that membranes 3 and 6, when taken together for the reasons which have been explained earlier, appear to provide a complete statement of the holdings under the lordship and to be in accordance with the 1357–60 accounts, and that membranes 4 and 5 may be dated as indicated above.

Survival of these records

The roll which constitutes SC 11/897 is preserved in the Public Record Office, where the catalogue does not indicate from which official source it arrived there.[37] In view of the diverse nature and dates of the records which survive in this roll, it seems most likely that they came together in the early 1360s in the Black Prince's exchequer where the accounts of Macclesfield and Longdendale were dealt with, possibly at Chester. While there is no direct evidence as to how that came about, possibilities may be suggested.

It has been made clear above that membranes 3, 6 and 7 were written as part of the process of making the extent from the evidence taken by John de Delves and John de Brunham in January 1360, and were the rough sheets from which the final copy of that extent would be made. When the lordship of Longdendale was farmed to Sir William Caryngton at Lady Day 1361 that fair copy would presumably have been passed to him with the lordship, and these rough sheets would have remained behind in the exchequer, as might also membranes 1 and 2, particularly since m. 2 has on its dorse an unconnected list likely to have been made there.

---

37 The P.R.O. online catalogue (PROCAT) lists the scope and content of class SC 11 as: 'Various manorial survey documents for crown lands, property which had passed into crown lands, ... or property which had been the subject of an official enquiry. ...

   The series was formerly known as Rentals and Surveys (General Series), Rolls. It was created artificially from records taken from three key Exchequer sources during the late nineteenth century, namely, Miscellanea from the Queen's Remembrancer's Office, the Treasury of the Receipt of the Exchequer and the Augmentation Office. Some records were also taken from those of the Palatinate of Chester.'

Membranes 4 and 5 (or the exemplars from which they were copied) on the other hand appear to have been made early in Sir William's tenure and presumably by or for his officials, recording in two stages the situation as it had been affected since the summer of 1361. When Sir William's farm of the lordship was suspended in 1366 he appears to have handed over to Adam de Kyngeslegh various records from which he in turn was able to construct a new rental. Those records may very probably have included membranes 4 and 5 of this roll (or their exemplars), but when the lordship was handed back to Sir William in 1368 it would presumably have been Adam de Kyngeslegh's up-to-date rental that would then have been handed over, perhaps together with the extent of 1360 and any other official records, leaving these membranes 4 and 5 at the exchequer. It seems that the officials wished and perhaps needed to keep such records in reserve, in case it should again be necessary to take over the lordship, and from then the roll, perhaps originally including other membranes, was passed down.

Such a theory may explain why what survives is a collection of preparatory and informal material and not either the final authoritative extent based on membranes 6 and 7 or Adam de Kyngeslegh's rental. It may be presumed that on 28 November 1374 the authoritative records would have been handed over with the lordship to Maud Holland and her husband John, Lord Lovel of Titchmarsh. The editor is unaware of where that family's archives now are, or if they survive.

Longdendale at a time of change
The rather strange gathering of documents which survives in the roll SC 11/897 illuminates in various ways a somewhat remote part of Cheshire at a time of considerable change. The highest-status structure in the lordship, Buckton Castle, which had been constructed in the late Norman period, doubtless with a view to exercising military control, was already a worthless ruin. The manor at which boon services were to be provided was already let at farm, and those services were regularly commuted for cash payments. In January 1360 the results of the Black Death of 1348 were still to be seen in the several properties, some not inconsiderable, which were 'in decay' or fallow for lack of tenants. The lordship had been escheated into the Black Prince's hands as a result of technical irregularity in being passed from father to son in an unauthorised manner. Then the authorities took the decision to farm out the lordship to one of the Black Prince's trusted retainers. Very soon after he took control pestilence struck again, apparently two years in succession, and he fell increasingly into arrears. After five years the lordship was once more taken into the hands of the prince's officials.

Such are the bare facts of the situation. What is presented in these records consists largely of names and figures, or routine statements of who held what property by what rents and services. All that is very formal, abstract, detached; but the names represent people, the inhabitants of the lordship, and the rents or services they rendered very often their livelihoods. The need for a new rental or a new extent, and some of the changes of names, or the disappearance of some names, from membranes 3, 6 and 7 to membranes 4 and 5 represent death and bereavement, possibly in the horrific circumstances of plague. It is difficult to personalise those cold statistics, but perhaps one Tintwistle family may assist us. In January 1360 the Tintwistle jury reported all the following concerning the family of a man whose name appears only in the genitive case as *Doke*:

6.16 *And that Magot Dok's wife holds at will three burgages and renders yearly at the same terms 2s.*
6.22 *And that Magot Dok's wife holds one croft and renders yearly 6d.*
6.23 *Item, the same Magot holds one toft in fee and renders to the lord yearly 6d.*
6.26 *Item, Magot Dok's wife holds one burgage and renders yearly 12d.*
6.26b *Item* [[*the same Mag holds le Smolterhouses which were John son of William de Hyde's and renders yearly 12d.*]] (This entry was deleted here because it was included in another entry below.)
6.24 *Item, Robert Dok's son holds one toft in fee and renders yearly 6d.*

Notwithstanding the fact that Magot's husband may be presumed to be deceased, there are signs here of a not inconsiderable enterprise to support the occupation of four burgages (each of which might normally suffice for a burgess's household), one toft, one croft and *le Smolterhouses* with the metalworking industry they apparently housed. This last item ought to have been subsumed within another entry, and tantalisingly vanishes from the record. Within eighteen months pestilence struck again. Set out below are the situations revealed in membranes 4 and 5 in the order of the manuscripts, which indeed seems likely to be the historical order. First from m. 4, of Martinmas (11 November), perhaps 1361:

4.41 *From Magot wife of Robert Dokeson* — 2s. 3d.
4.42 *From Robert Dokeson for a burgage* — 3d.

Here the first Magot's daughter-in-law, another Magot, appears to be paying the half-yearly rents for the burgages, croft and toft which her mother-in-law held in January 1360, plus 3d. which might possibly be part of the rent of *le Smolterhouses*, and Robert the half-year's rent of his own toft. One may only speculate as to the circumstances in which the husband made one payment and his wife the other. Then from m. 5, how much later we do not know precisely, but almost certainly not before Pentecost (5 June) 1362:

5.05 *From Mag' Dok's daughter from rent at the same terms* — 2s.
5.07 *From Mag' Dok's daughter for a burgage* — 12d.

Here is now no mention of either Robert or his wife. Dok's daughter, another Mag', now pays the annual rent of the three burgages which her father's widow held at will in **6.16**, and of the other burgage which she held (perhaps in fee) in **6.26**, but here is no sign of either her other ancillary properties or Robert's toft. We have no way of knowing how much suffering and loss of life these bare records conceal, but some consolation at least may be found in the mention in the 1408 Rental of Longdendale (MS. Harl. 2039, f. 113) of two men there named Robert Dooke the elder, perhaps a childhood survivor of these years, and Robert his son. See Prosopographical Index.

Publication

During its last years (1976-78) *The Cheshire Sheaf*, 5th series, carried in instalments in several issues (item nos. 57, 68, 83, 98, 104, 116, 121, 126, 131) a translation of *The Extent of Longdendale 1360* with introduction and notes by P.H.W. Booth, J.H. Harrop and S.A. Harrop. This collaborative enterprise was based on a transcript by Paul Booth, translation by John Harrop and notes to which all contributed, with historical input particularly from Paul Booth, and local input particularly from Sylvia Harrop. Unfortunately, the contributors were not afforded any opportunity of proof-reading, and in view of the unfamiliarity of the subject-matter to the type-setters it is not surprising that numerous errors and misunderstandings crept in and were printed uncorrected. *The Cheshire Sheaf* ceased publication before the contributors could either properly complete their task or supply lists of corrigenda. An unfortunate consequence of this state of affairs has been that more recent scholars working in the area have sometimes made use of less than satisfactory material. Since that first limited and rather disappointing publication, not only has our understanding of various particulars in the record developed, but also in recent years for this edition John Harrop has collated the transcript, and by the extensive use of ultra-violet light wherever necessary has recovered much that was previously unread, particularly m. 1 and m. 7d, filling many lacunae and establishing or correcting readings in many doubtful cases, has revised the translation and notes, and has compiled the Tables, Appendix and Prosopography. In doing so he has been particularly grateful to have had full access to Paul Booth's notes on the Longdendale and Macclesfield accounts and the benefit of his advice on many particular points.

Editorial conventions

The annotated text and translation are presented below on facing pages. **The text** has in general been printed as it was left to be read, words contracted or suspended in customary form having been extended as tittles, context and syntax require, with details of insertions and deletions usually provided in the footnotes. A few deleted entries of significant content have been printed in situ between double square brackets [[abc]]. In conformity with other volumes in this series the differing forms of the Latin letter U (i.e. *u* and *v*) have been printed as *u* when a vowel and *v* when a consonant. Readers are advised that this practice, first proposed by the humanist poet and spelling reformer Giangiorgio Trissino about 1520, although followed in the 1520s by the Roman printer Arrighi,[38] did not generally catch on at that time, but became common practice in print only after 1600, and does not in any way represent the normal medieval usage followed by the scribes of these records, which may be briefly illustrated by the original use in *per seruicia inueniendi vnum hominem*, and *vnam lagenam ceruisie* in **3.05**. The Society's precedents have also been followed in the omission of the dots which some of the scribes frequently, but by no means consistently, inserted before and after Roman

---

38 S.H. Steinberg, *Five Hundred Years of Printing*, new edn revised by John Trevitt (The British Library, London, 1996), p. 31.

numerals. Thus in entry **3.16** the clerk's *.v. s. ij. d.* has been printed as *v s. ij d.* Vernacular words are printed in italics. In the text of the narrower membranes 1–5 the original line-structure has been represented, but in the case of the wider membranes 6 and 7, where the lines are far too long for that to be convenient, each entry has been started on a new line, and the line-endings of the original have been indicated by I and the lines numbered. For reference purposes each entry has been given a number printed in bold, such as **3.02**. Explanatory material and headings in italics have been supplied by the editors. In addition:

[abc]   indicates words or letters defective, damaged or not completely legible;
[.....]   words or letters completely lacking;
[[abc]]   words or letters deleted, usually by being struck through;
<abc>   words or letters inserted above the line;
(xyz)   suggested extension of a contracted form;
(...)   uncertain extension of a suspended word.

An apostrophe at the end of a place-name or surname represents a sign of suspension added at this period as a formality representing a notional Latin case-ending.

In the translation, for the benefit of local historians and genealogists as well as students of place-names, all place-names and surnames have been printed in their original spellings, with explanations either in brackets or in footnotes when required. Latin Christian names have usually been translated. Explanatory material and headings in italics have again been supplied. When required, the same conventional signs are used as in the text to indicate insertions, deletions, etc., as above.

Acknowledgements

The undersigned wishes to express gratitude first to Paul Booth not only for the original introduction, many years ago, to this fascinating record, but also for all his subsequent collaboration, encouragement and support:

To the staff of the Public Record Office, especially in both the Long Room at Chancery Lane and the Map Room at Kew, for their unfailing courtesy and helpfulness; and in particular to Dr David Crook and Dr Malcolm Mercer, for information on the provenance of the roll, and Michael Prater for help in the examination of the watermark in m. 5:

To the staff of the Department of Manuscripts at The British Library for their constant helpfulness and courtesy; and in particular to Dr Andrea Clarke for search guidance:

To Sandra Mather of the Geography Department, The University of Liverpool, for drawing the map for this volume; to Ian Qualtrough and Suzanne Yee in the same department for processing old transparencies; and to the staff of the Sydney Jones Library there for continual kindness and helpfulness:

To Dr Mike Nevell of the Field Archaeology Unit, Manchester University, and to Dr John Barnet, Senior Survey Archaeologist, Peak District National Park Authority, for archaeological information:

To many friends for various help and information, and in particular Dr Philip Morgan of Keele University, the late Mrs Phyllis Hill, Sue Brown and Peter Gaskins of the Ranulf Higden Society, Mrs Anne Read formerly of Leeds University, and W.R. Mitchell, Esq., M.B.E., of Giggleswick:

To Mrs Rachel McGuicken, also of the Ranulf Higden Society, for taking the photographs of Buckton Castle and permission to include them:

To the Record Society's General Editor, Dr Peter McNiven, for his helpfulness, patience, courtesy and outstanding attention to detail:

Last but far from least to my wife Sylvia, not only for all her contribution in the early stages of this enterprise, but also in recent months for her helpful reading of drafts of the Introduction, and for much necessary patience and encouragement.

Needless to say, what faults remain must be ascribed to:

John Harrop
Austwick, North Yorkshire, June 2004.

Abbreviations used in the Introduction, Notes and Prosopographical Index

Aikin	John Aikin, *A Description of the Country from Thirty to Forty Miles Round Manchester* (Manchester, 1795)
B.P.R.	M.C.B. Dawes, ed., *Register of Edward the Black Prince*, 4 vols (London, 1930-33)
CCCIR 1373	P.R.O. CHES 25/4, *County Court of Chester Indictments Roll (1354–77)*, m. 29, in a transcript kindly provided by Mrs Phyllis Hill of the Ranulf Higden Society.
ChAcc2	Booth, P.H.W. and Carr, A.D., eds, *Account of Master John de Burnham the Younger, Chamberlain of Chester ... 1361–62*, R.S.L.C., cxxv (1991)
C.P.R.	*Calendar of Patent Rolls*
D.K.R. 36	*Report of the Deputy Keeper of the Public Records, 36 (London, HMSO, 1875)*
D.M.L.	R.E. Latham et al., eds, *Dictionary of Medieval Latin from British Sources* (London, O.U.P. for The British Academy, 1975– [in progress])
Dodgson	J.McN. Dodgson, *The Place-Names of Cheshire*, 4 vols (Cambridge, 1970–72)
Earwaker	J.P. Earwaker, *East Cheshire Past and Present*, 2 vols (London, 1880)
Maccl. Acc.	Booth, P.H.W., ed., *Accounts of the Manor and Hundred of Macclesfield, Cheshire, Michaelmas 1361 to Michaelmas 1362*, R.S.L.C., cxxxviii (2003)
Nevell & Walker	Michael Nevell and John Walker, *Lands and Lordships in Tameside* (Tameside, 1998)
O.E.D.	J.A. Simpson & E.S.C. Weiner, eds, *Oxford English Dictionary*, 2nd edn (Oxford, 1989)
P.I.	Prosopographical Index
P.R.O.	Public Record Office

TABLE 1

Values of rents, works, etc. in the Longdendale accounts 1357–1361.

	1 Escheator 29 Sep 57 to 13 Sep 58.	2 Prestbury 13 Sep 58 to 3 Apr 59.	3 Tieu 3 Apr 59 to 29 Sep 59.	4 Tieu 29 Sep 59 to 29 Sep 60.	5 Tieu 29 Sep 60 to 26 Mar 61.
Rents					
Tintwistle etc.	£12 12s. 5d.	£7 6s. 2½d.	£6 6s. 2½d.	£12 12s. 5d.	£6 6s. 2½d.
Mottram	£3 15s. 7¼d.	£1 17s. 9⅝d.	£1 17s. 9⅝d.	£3 15s. 7¼d.	£2 1s. 3⅜d.
Godley	2d.	1d.	1d.	2d.	15s. 9¾d.
Gt. & Lt. Holyn	8s. 4d.	4s. 2d.	4s. 2d.	8s. 4d.	4s. 2d.
Matley	4s.	Omitted	Omitted	4s.	£1 2s.
Wardship				6s.	3s.
	£17 0s. 6¼d.	£8 8s. 3⅛d.	£8 8s. 3⅛d.	£17 6s. 6¼d.	£10 12s. 5⅞d.
Works					
Newton	5s. 6½d	5s. 6½d. + 5s. 6½d.	5s. 6½d.	11s. 1d.	5s. 6d.
Stayley	4s. 10½d.	4s. 10½d.	4s. 10½d.	9s. 9d.	4s. 10½d.
Stayley + Hattersley		6s. 7½d.			
Hattersley	1s. 9d.		1s. 9d.	3s. 6d.	1s. 9d.
Reveyeld & Ward	13s. 3½d.	6s. 8d.	6s. 8d.	R: 10s. W: 3s. 3½d.	6s. 8d.
Haghehag				NIL	
.	£1 5s. 5½d.	£1 11s.	18s. 10d.	£1 17s. 7½d.	18s. 10d.
Farm					
Mill & Stallage	£3	£1 10s.	£1 10s.	£3	£1 10s.
Fair (issues)	7s. 3d.		5s. 6½d.	7s. 8d.	NIL
	£3 7s. 3d.		£1 15s. 6½d.	£3 7s. 8d.	£1 10s.
Herbage/Agistment	£12	n/a	£12	£12	NIL
Fishery	———	———	———	6s. 8d	NIL
				£12 6s. 8d.	
Court Perquisites	6s. 1d.	£1 5s. 1d.	7s. 3d.	£1 13s. 1d.	6s. 8d.
Increase of Rent				£2 19s. 2¼d.	
Sum Total Receipt [STR 1358-59]	£33 19s. 3¾d.	£12 14s. 4⅛d.	£23 9s. 10⅝d. [£36 4s. 2¾d.]	£39 10s. 9d.	£13 7s. 11⅞d.

Sources: SC 6/802/15, m. 1; 6/802/17, m. 5; 6/803/1, m. 6; and 6/803/3, m. 5.

TABLE 2

Values of rents, works, etc. in the membranes of SC 11/897.

The figures in the table below have been extracted or compiled from the membranes.

	m. 2 [Valuation]	m. 4 [Rental]	m. 5 Extent	mm. 3/6 Extent 1360
Rents				
Tintwistle etc.	£12 12s. 5d.	£6 11s. 9d.	£11 18s. 4d.	£12 12s. 5d.
Mottram	£3 15s. 4¼d.	£1 12s. 5½d.	£3 9s. 11d.	£3 15s. 4¼d.
Godley	2d.		2d.	2d.
Gt. & Lt. Holyn	8s. 4d.	5s. 1d.	8s. 4d.	8s. 4d.
Matley	5s.	4s.	4s.	4s.
Wardship		6s.		
Works				
Newton	11s. 1d.		11s. 1d.	No price.
Stayley	13s. 1d.		13s. 1d.	No price.
Hattersley	3s.		3s.	No price.
Reveyeld & Ward	7s. 11¾d.	2s. 10¼d.	R: 10s.	8s.
Haghehag				No price.
Farm				
Mill & Stallage	£4		£4	
Fair (issues)				
Herbage/Agistment	£12		£12	£12
Fishery	6s. 8d.			6s. 8d.
Court Perquisites	£1 4s. 6d.		£1	
Sum Total	£36 7s. 7d.		£35 7s. 1d.	

TABLE 3

Values of rents, works, etc. in the Longdendale accounts 1366–1368.

	6 Kyngeslegh 25 Mar 66 to 26 Mar 67.		7 Scolehalgh 25 Mar 67 to 25 Mar 68.
Rents			
Tintwistle tenants	£1 0s. 9d.		£1 0s. 9d.
Tintwistle termors	£7 11s. 8d.		£7 11s. 8d.
Micklehurst & Littlehurst termors	£5 2s. 4d.		£5 2s. 4d.
Mottram freeholders	15s.		15s.
Mottram termors	£3 18s. 2d.		£3 18s. 2d.
Gt Hollingworth freeholders	12s. 4d.		12s. 4d.
Godley free rent	2d.		2d.
Matley free rent	4s.		4s.
	£19 4s. 5d.		£19 4s. 5d.
Works			
Newton	11s. 1d.		11s. 1d.
Hattersley	3s. 6d.		3s. 6d.
Stayley	9s. 9d.		9s. 9d.
Reveyeld	10s.		10s.
Ward	3s. 4d.		3s. 4d.
Haghehag	NIL		NIL
	£1 17s. 8d.		£1 17s. 8d.
Issues of the Mill, Stallage, Fairs & Fishery			
Mill of Tintwistle (in hands *)	25s. 2½d.	(Wm. Milner)	10s.
(farmed to Robt. Smith from 29 Sept. 67)			15s.
Stallage (issues Lady Day – Michaelmas)	3s. 9d.		
Farm of the stallage	5s.		10s.
Toll of Tintwistle fair (issues)	13s. 4d.	(farm)	13s. 4d.
Fishery of Mersey & Edrow	NIL *		NIL *
	£2 7s. 4d.		£2 8s. 4d.
* (lack of farmers)			
Agistment all Longdendale lands			
(farmed to William Geffreu *et soc.*)	£13 6s. 8d.		£13 6s. 8d.
Perquisites of Courts			
Tintwistle	15s. 5d.		}*No details*
Mottram	2s. 3d.		
	18s. 4d.		£2 1s. 3d.
Escheats			
Moiety of the vill of Matley	£2 10s.		£2 10s.
Land of Henry, son of Wm Mattelegh	6s.		6s.
	£2 16s.		£2 16s.
Sum Total Receipt	£40 10s. 5d.		£41 14s. 4d.

Sources: SC 6/803/13, m. 3 and m. 4.

Notes and comments on the Tables

TABLE 1

1 Escheator's Account, 29 September 1357 – 13 September 1358
Under **Works** the ploughing/reaping/customary works due from Newton, Stayley and Hattersley are for one term only, namely ploughing due at Lady Day, but the Reveyeld & Ward figures are whole year's payments at the normal terms of Martinmas and Pentecost. From the extent (cf. **5.55–57** below) we may understand that the Hattersley figure for works includes a component for Haghehag.

2 Prestbury's Account, 13 September 1358 – 3 April 1359
Under **Rents** the £7 6s. 2½d., clearly written in the manuscripts, for Tintwistle etc. (i.e. Tintwistle, Arnfield, Littlehurst and Micklehurst) appears from the total to be a scribal error for £6 6s. 2½d. Matley is this time omitted from both the Rents list and the total.

Under **Works** two payments each appear from Newton and Stayley, but only one from Hattersley, yet the £1 11s. total is correct only if it included another 1s. 9d. from Hattersley. The Hattersley figure again (as customarily) includes a component for Haghehag. The period of this account included Michaelmas and Martinmas 1358 and Lady Day 1359, and the figure for Reveyeld and Ward presumably accounted for a rent that had come in at Martinmas 1358.

No figure is recorded for the farm of the **Herbage** or **Agistment**, which at this period was paid on St Bartholomew's Day, 24 August.

3 Tieu's Account, 3 April 1359 – 29 September 1359
This appears to be correct. Once again Matley is omitted from both the Rents list and the total. In this account the Hattersley figure for Works explicitly includes 'haghhagh'.

4 Tieu's Account, 29 September 1359 – 29 September 1360
This also appears to be correct. Note that Matley is now expressly included among the Rents. The NIL for Haghehag is explained by a statement that it was farmed with the agistment below.

Note that the farm of the **Fishery** of 'Merse' to Peter Arderne appears here for the first time. Cf. the extent entry **6.65** below.

The entry **Increase of Rent** £2 19s. 2¼d. deserves further explanation. It includes a rent of 5s. for a piece of ground in Mottram called 'Prestfeld', and 2s. for two pieces of meadow land in Woolley farmed this year, none of which is named in the membranes of SC 11/897, and which were presumably granted after the evidence for the 1360 extent was taken. Also included are 31s. 5½d. from the custody of the land of the heir of Geoffrey de Honford, 8¾d. from his free rent, and 20s. from half the manor of Matley, in the lord's hands because of John de Hyde's forfeiture, outlawed for the murder of Geoffrey de Honford. It is possible that the events underlying this entry explain the absence of mention of Matley from the previous accounts.

5 Tieu's Account, 29 September 1360 – 26 March 1361

In this half-year's account under **Rents** the figure of £2 1s. 3⅝d. for free tenants and tenants at will in Mottram now includes the rents of lands at Prestfeld and Woolley which were mentioned under 'Increase of Rent' in the previous account, the 15s. 9¾d. from similar tenants in Godley includes the rent from the land of the heir of Geoffrey de Honford also mentioned above, and the £1 2s. from Matley now includes 20s. for John de Hyde's lands now leased to the tenants of the township.

It may be noted that the sums under **Works** follow the earlier precedents, with Stayley still at 4s. 10½d. In this account haghehag is simply not mentioned. The works total is however incorrect and ought to have read 18s. 9½d.

There were no issues from the **Fair** since there had been no fair during the period of the account, nothing from **Agistment** since there had been no term in the period of the account, or from the **Fishery**, both manuscripts SC 6/803/3 and 6/803/4 containing at this point the note *pro defectu firmar'*, 'for lack of a farmer'. Under **Perquisites of Courts** Tintwistle had yielded 5s. 3d., and Mottram 1s. 5d.

TABLE 2

m. 2 [Valuation]

The Mottram valuation of £3 15s. 4¼d. appears to derive from membranes 3 and 6, for the accounts have £3 15s. 7¼d.

The Matley valuation of 5s. (**2.05** lists 5s. 4d. of which 4d. for reveyeld and ward) differs from the usually-given figure of 4s. The discrepancy may be explained by the fact that in the 1361–62 account (SC 6/803/5, m. 1d.) '12d. from works of the mill' appears for the first time as part of the 'Rents of Assise' from Matley. Those works had been mentioned in the rents section of the accounts for 1359–60 (SC 6/802/17, m. 5) and Michaelmas 1360 to Lady Day 1361 (SC 6/803/3, m. 5) but not accounted for in that section. In the Bailiff's account for 1366–67 (SC 6/803/13, m. 3), however, the free rent of Matley was again given as 4s.

The Stayley figure of 13s. 1d. representing works and services (cf. **5.53** below) may derive from the 1359–60 account, since this figure does not appear in the accounts for this period until it is mentioned under 'Respites' at the end of that account.

The figure of £4 for the farm of the mill and stallage (also found in **5.41** below) is difficult to explain since the figure in the accounts is consistently £3. Even if it was meant to include an additional sum for the issues of the annual fair it seems excessive, since during the period under consideration that produced only an amount varying between 5s. 6½d. and 7s. 8d.

The figure of 6s. 8d. for the farm of the fishery derives from membrane 6 (cf. **6.65** below where it is described as farmed to Peter Arden from Michaelmas 1359) or from the 1359–60 account, though it should be noted that during the next account (Michaelmas 1360 to Lady Day 1361) the fishery was not farmed.

From the evidence cited above, this membrane may thus be dated not before January 1360, and in view of the citation of evidence from the Respites of 1360, and of the 5s. rent from Matley, probably after the 1359–60 account.

m. 4 [Rental]
This membrane was clearly copied mainly from a Martinmas rental, though not all the payments recorded were half-yearly amounts. The majority of the receipts recorded in this membrane are explained by jurors' statements in membranes 3, 6 and 7.

The Tintwistle etc. (i.e. including Arnfield, Micklehurst and Littlehurst) rent of £6 11s. 9d., which we have derived from **4.27–54** (£6 7s. 9d.) and **4.69** (4s.) is difficult to reconcile with either the accounts or membranes 2 or 3/6, though the difficulty may be partly explained by the fact that entry **4.43** records a whole year's payment of 14s. 5d. from land of John de Hyde. It should be noted that the rents recorded from tenants of Micklehurst and Littlehurst (**4.50–54**) amount to £2 4s. 3½d., which would produce an annual rent of £4 8s. 7d., an increase on the £4 6s. 8d. or 6½ marks of **5.38** and **6.37**, though not as much as the £5 2s. 4d. shown in the 1366–68 accounts: see Table 3, p. xl and Introduction above, p. xix. It may also be noted that m. 4 records 23 rent receipts from Tintwistle and Arnfield, whereas mm. 3/6 have no fewer than 37 entries. From Mottram m. 4 records 14 rent receipts, whereas mm. 3/6 list 19 tenancies. See Appendix, pp. 74ff.

A similar difficulty arises with the Great and Little Hollingworth rent of 5s. 1d., which we have derived from **4.56–4.61** and **4.70**, and which if for Martinmas term only would suggest an annual rent of 10s. 2d., since the other membranes and the 1357–60 accounts have consistent annual rents of 8s. 4d., and the 1366–68 accounts rents of 12s. 4d. It is again significant that these entries include a number of otherwise unexplained payments, and while some of these may be for the whole year it is also clear that the membrane reveals a later situation than that in mm. 3/6. See Appendix, pp. 76f, 82.

For the mention in **4.68** of the wardship of the son of Robert de Holyn and the figure of 6s. (the only such mention in these membranes) and its relevance to the date of this membrane, see Introduction above, p. xix.

m. 5 Extent of Longdendale
This membrane is explicitly headed *Extenta de Longeden'*. It lists expected issues for the whole year.

The Tintwistle etc. rent total of £11 18s. 4d. is our sum of **5.27** and **5.38**, but **5.27** is 6d. less than the true total to that point; though even when that error is rectified this figure comes somewhat seriously short of the £12 12s. 5d. which appears as the Tintwistle rent both in the 1357–60 accounts and in membranes 2 and 3/6. It may however be significant that **5.27**, the total given here under Tintwistle, including Arnfield but not including Micklehurst and Littlehurst, appears in the 1366–68 accounts as the rent of 'termors' in the same township. From Tintwistle m. 5 lists 23 entries only, whereas m. 6 has 37.

Similarly, the Mottram rent of £3 9s. 11d., our sum of **5.37** and **5.47–50**, is difficult to reconcile with the £3 15s. 7¼d. in the accounts. As with Tintwistle, there is a reduction in the number of entries, m. 5 having 12 only by comparison with the 19 distinct tenancies listed in mm. 3 and 6 supported by 7.

It is significant that the value given to the rents and services due from Stayley appears in **5.53** as 13s. 1d., a figure which as mentioned above under m. 2 first appeared not as 'Rent' but under 'Respites' in the 1360 account.

The value of works and services due from Hattersley, including 'haghehag', is here given as 3s., whereas in the accounts it consistently appeared as 3s. 6d.

The Reveyeld figure of 10s. appears to derive from the accounts, and particularly the sum required there to be repaid annually to the lord of Macclesfield, rather than from a total of the payments due from the various tenants.

The annual sum for the farm of the mill and stallage is given as £4, whereas in the 1357–60 accounts it consistently appears as £3, and the 1366–68 accounts present a less prosperous situation. See above under m. 2.

The partly defective final sum total should amount to £34 17s. 11d.

For the date of this extent see Introduction above, pp. xviii, xxf.

mm. 3/6 Extent of Longdendale 1360

As explained earlier in this Introduction, pp. xvf., xxii, m. 3 is the first membrane of a very rough working draft of the extent which was made in January 1360 from the evidence given by named jurors, apparently continued on m. 6, which includes also evidence relating to Tintwistle given by a second jury. These two membranes (m. 3 and m. 6) taken together appear to provide a complete statement of the tenancies in the lordship of Longdendale at that date, with no apparent omissions.

These membranes contain no manor or township totals, so for purposes of direct tabular comparison the figures given for **Rents** have been compiled from the individual statements as follows: Tintwistle with Arnfield, Micklehurst and Littlehurst from **6.08–47**; Mottram from **3.14–18**, **6.02–03**, **6.48–60**; Godley from **3.11**; Great and Little Hollingworth from **6.04–07**; Matley from **3.08**.

Most of the **Works** due from each tenant are described in detail in these membranes, but apart from the undescribed Reveyeld and Ward no monetary value is attributed to them. Note that the total of both such payments in these membranes amounts to 8s. only, while in the 1357–60 accounts 10s. for Reveyeld was repaid annually to the lord of Macclesfield, and in 1359–60 the figure for Ward is given separately as 3s. 3½d.

The section which in the accounts is headed **Herbage/Agistment** etc., is to be found in **6.63–64**, with no evident mention of the fair, which in the accounts was in any case a matter of the actual issues of that year's fair. The farm of the **Fishery** is mentioned in **6.65**.

TABLE 3

6 Kyngeslegh's Account, 25 March 1366 – 6 March 1367 and
7 Scolehalgh's Account, 25 March 1367 – 25 March 1368

It will be immediately apparent that the entries under **Rents** in both these accounts have been differently categorised from the pre-1361 accounts, with explicit reference to 'termors', in which connection Kyngeslegh cites the rental made by himself 'in accordance with the demise of the lordship by Sir William Carington, late farmer'.

The figure of £7 11s. 8d. for Tintwistle termors (which must have included tenants of burgages, whether 'in fee' or 'at will') appears as the Tintwistle total in the m. 5 extent at entry **5.27** below. It is notable that the rent of the tenants-at-will (now also called 'termors') of Micklehurst and Littlehurst, which in **5.38** and **6.47** below was £4 6s. 8d., and in **4.50–54** for Martinmas term £2 4s. 3½d. (equivalent to an annual rent of £4 8s. 7d.), has by this stage grown to £5 2s. 4d. (an increase of 18%). It is difficult to reconcile precisely other Mottram and Tintwistle rents in these accounts with the membranes of SC 11/897.

The entries in both accounts under **Works** on the other hand appear to continue unaltered from Tieu's 1359-60 account, with Stayley again appearing as 9s. 9d., notwithstanding the entries of 13s. 1d. under 'Respites' in the 1359–60 account and in **5.53** below.

In the next section of the account more significant changes and difficulties appear. Tintwistle **Mill** was evidently in hands for lack of a farmer during the whole of the calendar year (Lady Day to Lady Day) 1366–67, during the first part of which, to Michaelmas 1366, the issues of the mill were sold wholesale (*sic vend' in grosso*) at a price of 7s. 2½d. (SC 6/803/12, m. 3). and by the following Lady Day the issues had risen to an annual total of a mere 25s. 2½d., also reported as sold wholesale by the bailiff's deputy (SC 6/803/13, m. 3). The mill was then held by the previous miller William Milner from Lady Day to Michaelmas 1367 before being farmed to Robert Smyth of Stayley for a period of six years at an annual rent of 30s. from Michaelmas 1367. From Lady Day to Michaelmas 1366 **Stallage** produced issues of 3s. 9d., but from that date it was farmed to Robert son of Thomas (1366) perhaps *alias* Robert Longdendale (1367) at an annual rate of 10s. The Toll of Tintwistle **Fair** appears to have produced issues of 13s. 4d. in 1366, but to have been farmed for that sum to an unidentified tenant the following year. The **Fishery** of Mersey & Etherow was evidently unproductive both years for lack of farmers. This may indicate that the authorities were expecting a higher rent than any prospective farmer was prepared to pay, and possibly that the fishery had proved less profitable than anticipated during Peter de Ardern's tenancy.

The rent of the **Agistment** of all Longdendale lands (farmed as before to William Geffreu and his companions) had now risen from £12 in the previous accounts and in entries **2.10**, **5.39–40** and **6.63–64** below to £13 6s. 8d. (an increase of just over 11%).

Both the items under **Escheats** have been mentioned above, in Tieu's 1359–60 account. The moiety of the vill of Matley appeared as 'Increase of Rent', and the land of Henry, son of William de Mattelegh under Rents as 'Wardship'. See notes above, p. xli. Both these properties are in these accounts recorded as having been demised to Margaret Hulm.

Plate 1
Buckton Castle from School Lane, Carrbrook.

Plate 2
Buckton Castle, looking towards the south gate from the SE ditch.
Plates 1 and 2 © Mrs Rachel McGuicken, July 2003.

Plate 3
Stayley Hall as it appeared in 1966.

Plate 4
Stayley Hall from the NE in 1966, revealing how the C17th stone cladding
covered the earlier timber-framed structure.

Plate 5
Newton Hall in 1968 when fire-damage had revealed the original cruck-framed structure. One pair of blades has been dated to the beginning of the fourteenth century.

Plate 6
The south end of Newton Hall in 1969 during restoration using medieval timber-framing methods.

Plate 7
Longdendale from below Mottram Church. Hollingworth and Woolley are in the middle distance, Tintwistle centre, and the hamlet of Arnfield in the valley at the left.

Plate 8
Mottram-in-Longdendale from above Roe Cross in 1966.

Plate 9
Longdendale from The Hague in Mottram.

Plate 10
Tintwistle seen from Hadfield on the other side of the valley.

Plate 11
The hamlet of Arnfield to the NW of Tintwistle.

Plate 12
Matley and Harrop Edge in 1971. In the foreground can be seen different sizes of ridge and furrow in the old arable land.

Plate 13
Salter's Brook: the old county boundary with Yorkshire at the eastern extremity of the lordship of Longdendale.

Plate 14
The old bridge over Salter's Brook on the pack-horse route through Longdendale into Yorkshire.

ANNOTATED TEXT AND
TRANSLATION OF
THE SEVEN MEMBRANES OF
P.R.O. SC 11/897

m. 1

[Parchment (flesh side) 22.4 cm. high × 6.0–7.7 cm. wide.]

This membrane is in very poor condition, completely illegible by normal light, and even under ultra-violet light it can be only partly read. It is written in a different hand from any of the remainder of the membranes. In most cases it is impossible to be certain of the case-endings of the Christian names on each line since they are generally suspended, and where filius *appears it is always written simply* fil.

1.01	Robertus de Padfeld
1.02	Filius Willelmi Wade
1.03	Robertus filius Symonis filii Rogeri
1.04	Henricus le tern[..]
1.05	Adam le botelir
1.06	[....] le Smyth
1.07	Robertus filius Coke
1.08	Johannes [........]
1.09	Willelmus le mulner
1.10	[....] filius [.....] de Godelegh
1.11	Johannes le Warde
1.12	Ricardus de Wolegh
1.13	Ade *(sic)* [...]ller
1.14	Thomas le Spener
1.15	Ricardus filius Thome Maykyn
1.16	Johannes de Bentelegh'
1.17	Thomas filius Adam *(sic)*
1.18	[....] Olde
1.19	[....] Ade
1.20	[...] filius [...]
1.21	[...] filius Broke
1.22	[...] filius eius
1.23	[...] filius Willelmi
1.24	Johannes filius eius
1.25	Johannes de Cnangreve[(a)]
1.26	[...] Hyrnet
1.27	[...] filius Ricardi
1.28	[... ... .]
1.29	[...] le [...]
1.30	[...] del Grene
1.31	[... .. ..]
1.32	[... .. ...]

(a) Or *Cnangrene*, or *Onangrene*, or *Onangreve*.

m. 1

LIST OF NAMES WITHOUT HEADING[1]

1.01	Robert de Padfeld (Padfield)
1.02	Son of William Wade
1.03	Robert son of Symon son of Roger
1.04	Henry le tern[..]
1.05	Adam le botelir (butler)
1.06	[....] le Smyth
1.07	Robert son of Cok(e)
1.08	John [........]
1.09	William le mulner
1.10	[....] son of [.....] de Godelegh (Godley)
1.11	John le Warde
1.12	Richard de Wolegh
1.13	of Adam (*sic*) [...]ller
1.14	Thomas le Spener
1.15	Richard son of Thomas Maykyn
1.16	John de Bentelegh'
1.17	Thomas son (of) Adam
1.18	[....] Olde
1.19	[....] of Adam
1.20	[...] son of [...]
1.21	[...] son of Brok(e)
1.22	[...] his son
1.23	[...] son of William
1.24	John his son
1.25	John de Cnangreve
1.26	[...] Hyrnet
1.27	[...] son of Richard
1.28	[... ... .]
1.29	[...] le [...]
1.30	[...] del Grene
1.31	[... .. ..]
1.32	[... .. ...]

1 All persons whose names appear in these manuscripts are listed, and as far as possible identified, with full cross-references and other relevant information, in the Prosopographical Index, hereafter cited as P.I.

m. 1

1.33	[... .. ..]
1.34	[...] filius [......]
1.35	[...] le Fysse
1.36	[...] le mulner de Cyntyll'
1.37	[...] filius Petri de Benfort[b]

m. 1d
[Written (towards the foot of the hair side) in a different hand from the recto.]

It is not certain that this heading refers to the list of names on the other side of the membrane, though if it does that list would be relevant to the valuation of the lordship.

Nomina transgressorum[c] in aqua de Longedendale

Rest of membrane blank.

(b) Or *Beufort*, or *Wenfort*.
(c) ms. *transgr'*

m. 1

    1.33   [... .. ….......]
    1.34   […] son of [......]
    1.35   […] le Fysse
    1.36   […] le mulner de Cyntyll'
    1.37   […] son of Peter de Benfort

m. 1d

Names of trespassers in the water of Longdendale.[2]

---

2   It is possible (though it is impossible to be certain) that this is the heading for the list in a different hand on the other side of this membrane. A list of trespassers might form part of the background material for an extent by indicating potential revenue from amercements or licences.

m. 2
[Parchment (rather rough, hair side) 29.4 cm. high × 4.0–6.5 cm. wide.]

SUMMARY VALUATION OF COMPONENT PARTS OF THE LORDSHIP OF LONGDENDALE without heading or date.

			<r + [w]>[(d)]
2.01	Tyng'	xij li. xiij s. v d.	<unde xij […]>
2.02	Mottrum	lxxvij s. vij d.	<ij s. ij d. ob. qu.>
2.03	Neuton'	xj s. j d.	
2.04	Stavel'	xiij s. j d.	
2.05	Mattel'	v s. iiij d.	<iiij d.>
2.06	Godl'	ij d.	
2.07	Hattresl'	iij s. ix d.	<ix d.>
2.08	Magna Holyn'	iiij s. ij d.	<x d.>
2.09	Parva Holyn'	vij s. x d.	<ij s. x d.>
2.10	Longeden'	xij li.	
2.11	Molendin'	iiij li.	

(d) Sc. *reveyeld + ward'*. This appears to be inserted after either *unde* or at the line end, and to be intended to serve as the heading for the figures in the column below.

m. 2

SUMMARY VALUATION OF COMPONENT PARTS OF THE LORDSHIP OF LONGDENDALE without heading or date.[3]

					r + [w][4]
					of which 12 [..][6]
2.01	Tyng' (Tintwistle)	£12	13s.	5d.[5]	
2.02	Mottrum (Mottram)		77s.	7d.[5]	<2 s. 2¾d .>[6]
2.03	Neuton' (Newton)		11s.	1d.[7]	
2.04	Stavel' (Stayley)		13s.	1d.[7]	
2.05	Mattel' (Matley)		5s.	4d.	<4d.>[8]
2.06	Godl' (Godley)			2d.[5]	
2.07	Hattresl' (Hattersley)		3s.	9d.[7]	<9d.>[9]
2.08	Great Holyn' (Hollingworth)		4s.	2d.[5]	<10d.>[10]
2.09	Little Holyn' (Hollingworth)		7s.	10d.[5]	<2s. 10d.>[11]
2.10	Longeden' (-dale)	£12.[12]			
2.11	Mill	£ 4.[13]			

3 Note that the figures in the main column on this page include the amounts shown on the right-hand side. The figures in this list have been compared with those in the accounts for the lordship of Longdendale for 1357–61 and 1366–68 (SC 6/802/15, m. 1; 6/802/17, m. 5; 6/803/1, m. 6; 6/803/3, m. 5; 6/803/13, m. 3 and m. 4) as indicated below. See Introduction, pp. xxxf. and Tables with the accompanying notes, pp. xxxviiif.

4 This should be read as *reveyeld and ward* and appears to be the heading for the figures interlineated below. It is perhaps significant that the total of reveyeld and ward on this membrane amounts to 7s. 11¼d., where membranes 3 and 6 (on our reckoning) produce 8s., both significantly less than the figure of 10s. for reveyeld alone shown by the accounts as being repaid annually to the lord of Macclesfield. See Tables 1 and 3, pp. xxxviii, xl.

5 These figures are all rents, and may be compared with those in the accounts referred to above, viz:– Tintwistle £12 12s. 5d.; Mottram £3 15s. 7¼d.; Godley 2d.; Great and Little Hollingworth 8s. 4d.; Great and Little Matley 4s. See also Table 2, column 4, p. xxxix. The 5s. for Matley here may be explained by the fact that in the 1361–62 account (SC 6/803/5, m. 1d.) '12d. from works of the mill' appears for the first time as part of the 'Rents of Assise' from Matley. In the Bailiff's account for 1366–67, however, the free rent of Matley was again given as 4s.

6 In most cases these figures on the right-hand side correlate with statements in the remainder of the membranes relating to reveyeld and ward, as indicated below. Reveyeld and ward from Tintwistle and Arnfield amounts to 12d. in m. 6, though m. 4 (which appears to be later) has 7½d. for Martinmas term. The combined figure from Mottram in mm. 3/6 amounts to 2s. 3d., while m. 4 has a Martinmas figure of 1s. 4¾d.

7 These figures all refer to works and customs, comparable with the following figures in the 1357–60 accounts:- Newton 11s. 1d.; Stayley 9s. 9d.; Hattersley 3s. 6d. **2.07** appears also in **5.55–57**.

8 This is the total of reveyeld and ward mentioned under Matley in **3.06** and **4.64–65**.

9 This is the sum given for reveyeld and ward from Hattersley in **7.14**.

10 This is the total of reveyeld and ward from Great Hollingworth in **6.04** and **7.23**.

11 This is the total of reveyeld and ward from Little Hollingworth in **6.06–07** and **7.24–26**.

12 This figure presumably refers to the farm of the herbage or agistment of Longdendale, worth £12 in the 1357–61 accounts. Cf. **6.63**, the defective entry at **5.39–40**, and Tables, pp. xxxviii–xl.

13 This figure appears to be for the farm of the mill and stallage of Tintwistle and may perhaps be the source of **5.41**, since the 1357–61 accounts consistently have £3 annually.

m. 2

2.12	Piscari(a)	vj s. viij d.
2.13	Perquisita Curi(arum)	xxiiij s. vj d.
2.14	**Summa totalis**	xxxvj li. vij s. vij d.[e]

(e) *Summa totalis (xxv li. iij s. j d.)* first written struck through.

m. 2

2.12	Fishery	6s.	8d.[14]
2.13	Perquisites of Courts	24s.	6d.[15]
2.14	**Sum total**	£36 7s.	7d.[16]

14 This figure is for the farm of the fishery of Etherow leased to Peter de Arden in 1359–60. Cf. **6.65** and the 1359–60 accounts, where it is noted that the lease began at Michaelmas 1359. It was not, however, leased in the following year 'for lack of a farmer'.
15 The 1359–60 accounts mention two courts, at Tintwistle and Mottram, which yielded 28s. 10d. and 4s. 4d. respectively. Cf. **5.60**. See also Tables 1 and 3, pp. xxxviii, xl.
16 The annual figures for the lordship lie between £35 and £40. Cf. **5.62** and Introduction, pp. xiiif, xxxf, with Tables, pp. xxxviii–xl.

m. 2d

[Written on up-turned membrane, i.e. the other way up from the recto, and two-thirds down the available space, this flesh side being more polished than the other.]

LIST OF THE FORESTERS OF MACCLESFIELD

2d1	Thomas Fyton' de Gous'
2d2	Johannes de Sutton'
2d3	Edmundus de Dounes
2d4	Johannes filius Ricardi de Sutton'
2d5	Ricardus de Stanlegh'
2d6	Thomas de Worth'
2d7	Edmundus de Upton'

m. 2d

LIST OF THE FORESTERS OF MACCLESFIELD[17]

2d1	Thomas Fyton de Gous' (Gawsworth)[18]
2d2	John de Sutton[19]
2d3	Edmund de Dounes (Downes)[20]
2d4	John son of Richard de Sutton[21]
2d5	Richard de Stanlegh (Stanley)[22]
2d6	Thomas de Worth[23]
2d7	Edmund de Upton[24]

17 It is not clear why this list appears on this membrane, or when it was written. See Introduction, pp. xivf. It is interesting that this list contains only seven names, since there were eight forester-ships. The missing name is that of John de Pecton, whose family somehow acquired the Distelegh forestership in the second quarter of the fourteenth century, and who himself died in 1362: Earwaker, ii. 85. The omission may imply that this list dates from after John de Pecton's death.

18 Thomas Fyton was called 'Forester in Fee' in a land dispute in May 1354: *B.P.R.*, iii. 160. He appears to have inherited the Orreby forestership: Earwaker, ii. 550–1.

19 John de Sutton was succeeded as Forester of Macclesfield by his kinsman John son of Richard Sutton in 1362: *B.P.R.*, iii. 450–1. See below, note 21.

20 Edmund de Downes received his father's forestership in Macclesfield in 1344: *C.P.R. 1343–45*, p. 355.

21 The Suttons appear to have held two foresterships – one for lands in Disley, the other for lands in Sutton; the former held 'as of ancient tenure, in fee and inheritance', the latter held 'by deed of Earl Hugh'. There are two Suttons also in Earwaker's list of Macclesfield foresters, which he believes to date from about the end of the thirteenth century (Earwaker, ii. 6–7, 90, 439).

22 Called Forester of Macclesfield c. 1357: *B.P.R.*, iii. 253. He farmed the coalmines within the for-est for 8s. in 1360–61 (SC 6/803/3, m. 4). See also Earwaker, ii. 88–9.

23 About 1362 a certain William de Hulme obtained the forestership of Thomas de Worth from the Earl of Chester: ibid., p. 341. This list was probably written between John de Pecton's death and this event.

24 An Edmund Upton farmed the lands in Marple of Richard Vernon who was a ward in 1351 (SC 6/802/7, m.1). He appears to have taken over the Vernon forestership temporarily. See also Earwaker, ii. 50.

m. 3

[Parchment (flesh side) 29.7 cm. high × 9 cm. wide.]

Written on a piece of parchment which had previously been used in horizontal format for the beginning of a charter or similar document in Anglo-Norman.[f]

PRELIMINARY DRAFT OF THE EXTENT[g] *without heading or date.*

3.01

Robertus de Staveley	Juratus
Robertus de Neuton'	Juratus
Ricardus de Woley	Juratus
Willelmus Gybonsone[h]	Juratus
Radulfus de Woley	+
Ricardus de Dewisnape	Juratus
Robertus de Holynworth'	Juratus
Rogerus del Bothum	Juratus
Willelmus Geffrou	Juratus
Willelmus de Throntel'[i]	Juratus

(f) *[A] touz ceux que cestes lettres verrount ou orrount Willeam de Bottiler de Wemme le puisne.* This single line in a different hand and ink runs up the whole length of the left margin of m. 3 as it now is.

(g) An extent normally begins with a heading and date, with a note of who was conducting the investigation, followed by the names of the jury, who were sworn to tell the truth about the details which the extent would go on to list. The fact that an old piece of parchment was re-used, the absence of the preliminaries found at the beginning of m. 6 before the names of the jury here, and the cross by Ralph Woley's name all indicate that this membrane was a rough draft or working document.

(h) Or *Gybousone*, and so whenever the name appears.

(i) *Thornclyf* first written was struck through and *Throntel'* (for *Throntelegh*) written instead.

m. 3

PRELIMINARY DRAFT OF THE EXTENT without heading or date.[25]

3.01

Robert de Staveley[26]	sworn
Robert de Neuton[27]	sworn
Richard de Woley[28]	sworn
William Gybonsone[29]	sworn
Ralph de Woley[30]	+
Richard de Dewisnape[31]	sworn
Robert de Holynworth[32]	sworn
Roger del Bothum[33]	sworn
William Geffrou[34]	sworn
William de Throntel(egh)[35]	sworn

25 For all persons named in this membrane see P.I. In what is now the left margin of this draft the beginning of a charter or similar document in Anglo-Norman (for which the parchment had been previously intended) reads: *To all those who shall see or hear these letters, Willeam de Botiller de Wemme the younger...*

26 Holder of the manor of Stayley: see **3.04** & **7.27**. This jury was evidently composed of substantial tenants or their representatives.

27 Holder of the manor of Newton: see **3.05** & **7.03**.

28 Holder of one third of the manor of Little Hollingworth, presumably including the hamlet of Woolley in Hollingworth township on the Cheshire/Derbyshire border: see **6.05** & **7.24**.

29 This name is found in these membranes only in the lists of jurors here and in **6.01**, **7.01**. He may have represented Henry Gybon who held lands in Mottram: see **6.50**, and also **4.06–09**, **5.30** and P.I.

30 In 1349 Ralph de Woley (nephew of Richard) became possessed of lands in Broadbottom (see **3.17**, **5.48** & **7.19**) and these lands remained in the family until the sixteenth century at least. The cross by his name indicates that though summoned he did not appear. Earwaker, ii. 154; H.T. Milliken, *Saga of a Family* (London, 1967), pp. 2–3.

31 Holder of a messuage and half a bovate of land in Mottram: see **3.16** & **7.18**. His name may be from either Dewsnap in Hollingworth (Dodgson, i. 310), or the Dewsnap in Tintwistle (ibid., p. 327).

32 Robert de Holynworth may have appeared on this jury to represent not only John de Holynworth, holder of Great Hollingworth, but especially his own son Henry, then in wardship, holder of a fourth part of the township of Matley. He was later recorded as holder of land in Hollingworth: see **4.56–57**. See P.I.

33 Holder of the manors of Great and Little Arnfield (see **6.45–46**) and other lands. Possibly named from the place now called Botham's Hall at Broadbottom, S.W. of Mottram (Dodgson, i. 307).

34 Holder of a burgage and other lands in Tintwistle, later including Herstancloghous': see **6.19** and **5.24–25**. With others, William Geffrou farmed the agistment of Longdendale in 1358–60, 1366–68. (SC 6/802/17, m. 5, where he is called son of Geoffrey; 803/13, mm. 3 and 4.)

35 Holder of a burgage and valuable lands adjacent: see **6.41**. The name is given in various spellings in these membranes: see P.I. Dodgson, i. 309 identifies it as the modern Thorncliffe. He may have appeared on this jury to represent Christiana de Holynworth, holder of two thirds of Little Hollingworth and Thorncliffe, and whose son he may have been. See **4.71**.

m. 3

Johannes Lastles	Juratus
Willelmus del Fernylegh'	Juratus
Johannes Hobrode[j]	Juratus

3.02 qui dicunt super sacramentum suum quod est ibi
unum Castrum dirutum vocatum Buckeden'
et nullius valoris.   **3.03** Item, est ibi una aula,[k] una
Camera [l] et una Capella
que dimittuntur ad firmam ut infra.   **3.04** Item,
dicunt quod Robertus de Stavelegh' tenet
Manerium de Stavelegh' de domino de
Long' per servicium militare, et idem Robertus
habet diem ad ostendendum per que servicia
tenet idem Manerium.   **3.05** Item, Robertus de Neuton'
tenet Manerium de Neuton' per servicium Militare
et per servicia inveniendi pro quolibet tenente suo
terminario unum hominem per iij dies[m] tempore autumpnali
ad unum Pastum per diem, videlicet panem, butirum et lac,[n] apud Manerium
de Arnefeld' quod dimittitur ad firmam,
et tempore quadragesimali pro quolibet tenente predicto
unam carucam per tres dies ad unum
pastum per diem, videlicet pro una caruca

(j)   *de Brod* first written was struck through and *Hobrode* written instead. From **3.02** onwards, the
        text is written in a second, smaller hand (hand 2), comparable with that of **6.08**ff. and **m. 7d**.
(k)   *una aula* interlineated.
(l)   *in manu domini* struck through.
(m) *per iij dies* interlineated.
(n)   *videlicet panem butirum et lac* interlineated.

m. 3

John Lastles[36]	sworn
William del Fernylegh[37]	sworn
John Hobrode[38]	sworn

3.02 who say upon their oath that there is there one ruined castle called Buckeden (Buckton) and of no value.[39]   **3.03** Item, there is there one hall, one chamber and one chapel which are let at fixed rent as below.[40]

[Stayley]

3.04 Item, they say that Robert de Stavelegh holds the manor of Stavelegh from the lord of Longdendale by knight service, and the same Robert has a day for showing by what services he holds the same manor.[41]

[Newton]

3.05 Item, Robert de Neuton holds the manor of Neuton by knight service and by the services of finding for every termor tenant[42] of his one man for 3 days at harvest time at one meal per day, that is to say bread, butter and milk, at the manor of Arnefeld[43] which is let at fixed rent, and in Lenten time for every aforesaid tenant one plough for three days at one meal per day, that is to say for one plough

---

36 One of the joint tenants of Micklehurst and Littlehurst: see **6.47**. Possibly connected with the Astle or Asthulle family of Chelford or Wilmslow. His name was not included among the tenants listed in the Martinmas rental of m. 4.

37 Another of the joint tenants of Micklehurst and Littlehurst: see **6.47**. He may take his name from the Fern Lee at Greenfield, West Yorkshire, only a couple of miles N.E. of Micklehurst, or possibly from the Fernilee in the Goyt Valley, S. of Whaley Bridge.

38 Holder of *le Wallecroft* and other lands in Tintwistle: see **6.34** and **6.39–40**.

39 See **7.02**. Buckton is a hill 1,126 ft. high surmounted by a medieval ring-motte overlooking the valley of the river Tame, and was in Tintwistle township (O.S. map ref. SD 989016). For fuller discussion of this site see Nevell & Walker *passim*, and especially pp. 60–4, where it is referred to as the highest status site in the Tameside area.

40 See **7.02b**. After the castle the next in status to be listed might be expected to be the principal manor of the lordship, though the complex of buildings described here is now leased out. The only manor on lease in these manuscripts is Arnfield, which may be intended here: see **3.05** below (cf. the defective **7.03**) from which it is clear that the boon services of ploughing and reaping referred to were to be performed there. See n. 43 below. The earl of Chester's manor house at Tintwistle is mentioned in Isabel de Stokeport's Inquisition Post Mortem of 1370 (Earwaker, ii. 153). In the County Court of Chester Indictments Roll, 1354–77 (CHES 25/4), m. 29, hereafter cited as CCCIR 1373, presentments were made against Sir William Caryngton, then farmer of the lordship of Longdendale, for demolishing between the years 1361 and 1373 *inter alia* a hall and a chamber in Longdendale worth 50s. each; a chapel in Tintwistle worth 40s.; and a hall and chamber in Tintwistle worth £10, formerly William de Hyde's. (Transcript provided by the late Mrs Phyllis Hill of the Ranulf Higden Society.)

41 See **7.27** and **5.53**. For the manor of Stayley see Earwaker, ii. 165ff., and Nevell & Walker, *passim*.

42 I.e. a tenant holding for a number of years.

43 I.e. Arnfield, cf. Aikin, p. 469; Earwaker, ii. 171. It is noteworthy that Arnfield is here described as a manor, and that the boon services were rendered here (or more properly had been, since they were now commuted for cash payments), which suggests that this may originally have been the chief manor of the lordship. In that case, the 'hall, chamber and chapel' of **3.03** may have been situated here. Their subsequent disappearance may have been due to the actions for which Sir William Caryngton was indicted in 1373, as mentioned above in note 40. According to **6.45–46** Roger del Bothum held at will both Great and Little Arnfield.

m. 3

per diem, vj kakes aven(e), vj allec(ia)
et unam lagenam Cervisie, et dominus inveniet
eis foragium et unam domum^(o) pro animalibus caruce ad
custus dictorum tenentium.   **3.06** Item quod W. de Hyde
tenuit medietatem manerij de Mattelegh' *<drive & lede>*^(p)
et obijt inde seisitus, et descendit ius
eiusdem medietatis Ricardo filio ipsius
Willelmi, et idem R(icardus) obijt inde seisitus
et ius eiusdem medietatis descendit Johanni
fratri eiusdem Ricardi ^(q)
et Johannes de Hyde, Chivaler, tenet eandem
medietatem quo iure nesciunt. Et tenetur
eadem medietas de domino per servicium militare.
Et dat pro revegald' iij d. Et pro
ward' j d.

(o) *et unam domum* interlineated.
(p) *drive & lede* interlineated above *Mattelegh'*, without 'caret'.
(q) *et idem Johannes tenet* next written struck through.

m. 3

per day 6 oat cakes,[44] 6 herrings[45] and one gallon of ale, and the lord will find for them forage and a house for the plough animals at the costs of the said tenants.[46]
[Matley]
3.06 Item, that W(illiam) de Hyde held half of the manor of Mattelegh <drive and lead>[47] and died seised of it, and the right to the same half descended to Richard son of that William, and the same Richard died seised of it, and the right to the same half descended to John brother of the same Richard, and John de Hyde, knight, holds the same half by what right they do not know.[48] And the same half is held from the lord by knight service. And it gives for revegald 3d.[49] And for ward 1d.[50]

---

44 Oatcakes (in parts of Lancashire much the same shape as elongated pitta bread, in the West Riding of Yorkshire resembling wash-leathers) continued to be traditional fare until the 1960s, and circular ones (about the size of a dinner plate) are still popularly produced in Derbyshire and Staffordshire. Aikin (p. 463) wrote significantly of Mottram in 1795: 'Oatcakes, leavened and baked thick, are the principal bread of the place.' Cf. Marie Hartley and Joan Ingilby, *Life & Tradition in the Yorkshire Dales* (London, 1968), pp. 21–8 and plates 34–41.

45 Presumably salted, and appropriate fare for Lent. They must have been brought up from the coast. The Church's dietary rules for fast days and Lent required and produced a thriving trade in fish, though not always from the sea as here.

46 Cf. **7.03**. These services are not mentioned in Robert de Newton's Inquisition Post Mortem, 1362, which provides additional information on Robert's tenure (Earwaker, ii.161–3).

47 See **7.04**, sadly defective. The expression *drive & lede* written in English in this rough draft above *Mattelegh* appears again later in **6.06** (about Hollingworth). That expression is replaced in the parallel clause **7.25** by *makes suit to the lord's mill*. It may thus refer to the obligation to carry grain to and meal from the lord's mill. From **3.08** it appears that the mill in question was the one at Tintwistle, which was some distance from the settlement at Matley.

48 This statement may help to explain why by Pentecost (24 May) 1360 this half of Matley had been taken into the hands of the lord of Longdendale and leased at will to the tenants of the township for 40s. per annum (SC 6/802/17, m. 5.) See P.I. and Earwaker, ii. 157.

49 This vernacular word appears sometimes as *revegald*, sometimes *reveyeld*.

50 These customs, also payable in the manor of Macclesfield, were for services which are not precisely identified in the mss. See Introduction, pp. xxv–xxvi.

m. 3d   [The same way up as the recto (hair side).]

3.07 Item dicunt quod Johannes de Hyde tenet quartam partem Manerij de Mattel' per servicium militare.   **3.08** Item quod Henricus
filius Roberti de Holynworth tenet aliam quartam partem
eiusdem Manerij per idem servicium, et per servicium iiij s.
de toto Manerio, et per *Haghehag'*, ⁺ videlicet inve-
niendum vj homines per j diem sine pastu [r] ad faciendum hayam pro venacione
domini quolibet anno, et per servicium faciendi opus terrenum
ad molendinum de Tyngetwysell quociens opus
fuerit, et faciendi sectam ad Curiam de Mottrum,
et inveniendi duos Judices.   **3.09** Item quod Johannes de
Hyde tenet [s] medietatem Manerij de Godlegh', et
Howel ap Oweyn et fil(ius) W. de Tranemol
tenet quartam partem dicte ville, et filia et heres
Galfridi de Honford' tenet quartam partem eiusdem ville
et est infra etatem, videlicet iiij annorum, per servicium militare.
3.10 Item, Robertus le Ward de Godl' tenet in eadem
villa dimidiam carucatam terre et unum Mesuagium, an tenet
de domino an de aliis ignorant, set facit *Haghehag'* et opus molendini ut supra.   **3.11** Item quod Johannes
filius Johannis de Godl' de eadem tenet unum mesuagium
et xxiiij acras terre in eadem et reddit domino
de Longg'[t] j d. per annum et Johannes de Hyde

(r) *per j diem sine pastu* interlineated.
(s) *quart* struck through, *medietatem Manerij* struck through, *medietatem Manerij* interlineated
     above.
(t) Sc. *Longgedendale*.

m. 3d

3.07 Item, they say that John de Hyde[51] holds a quarter of the manor of Mattel' by knight service.

3.08 Item that Henry son of Robert de Holynworth holds the other quarter of the same manor by the same service and by the service of 4s. from the whole manor,[52] and by haghehag,[53] that is finding 6 men for 1 day without a meal in order to make a hay for the lord's venison each year, and by the service of making earthwork at Tintwistle mill whenever it shall be necessary, and of making suit at Mottram Court, and of finding two doomsmen.[54]

[Godley]

3.09 Item that John de Hyde[55] holds half the manor of Godlegh, and Howel ap Oweyn[56] and the son of W. de Tranemol (Tranmere)[57] holds a quarter of the said township, and the daughter and heiress of Geoffrey de Honford (Handforth)[58] holds a quarter of the same township and is under age, that is 4 years, by knight service.

3.10 Item, Robert le Ward de Godl' holds in the same township half a carucate of land and one messuage; they do not know whether he holds it from the lord or from others, but he does haghehag and work of the mill as above.[59]

3.11 Item that John son of John de Godl' of the same holds one messuage and 24 acres of land in the same and renders to the lord of Longg' 1d. a year and John de Hyde renders another penny for his holding in the same township.[60]

---

51 Sir John de Hyde, who in 1364 sold half the manor of Godley, a sixth of the manor of Newton, a quarter of the manor of Matley and other lands: see **7.05**, **3.06** with note 49, note 55 and P.I.

52 See **7.06** and **5.51**. The 1359/60 account indicates that at this time this Henry was a ward. See P.I.

53 This interesting service has not so far been encountered elsewhere in Cheshire, though a similar service is referred to in the Inquisition Post Mortem of Isabel de Stokeport, 1370, details of which are given below, p. 71, note 294. See also Nevell & Walker, pp. 53–7, which refers to a recently identified deer hay at The Hague in Mottram, which may have been the place where this service was performed.

54 See Introduction, p. xxv and **5.63** with note 182. In the 1361–62 account (SC 6/803/5, m. 1d.) there appears for the first time under 'Rents of Assise' from Matley *et ultra xij d. de operibus molendini*, 'and over and above 12d. from works of the mill'. In the Bailiff's account for 1366–67 the free rent of Matley was again given as 4s. For doomsmen see Introduction, p. xxv.

55 See **7.07**. In 1364 Sir John de Hyde sold this half of Godley and other lands including some in Mottram mentioned below to Richard son of Richard Mascy of Sale (Earwaker, ii. 157).

56 Howel ap Oweyn Voel was kinsman and heir of William Boydell in 1354. See P.I.

57 See **7.08**. William son of William de Tranemol was already married to Katherine daughter of Geoffrey de Honford by 1362 (both under age). See next note.

58 See **7.09**. In Robert de Newton's Inquisition Post Mortem of 1362 (Earwaker, ii. 161) Geoffrey de Honford was called Lord of Godley, and his daughter and heiress Katherine was already wife of William son of William de Tranemol. It appears that Sir John de Hyde was responsible for engineering the murder of Geoffrey de Honford, which was actually carried out by his son William, the servant Hugh Frenshie and John son of William de Hyde in or before 1359–60. The custody of the land of the heir of Geoffrey de Honford contributed 31s. 5½d. under 'Increase of rent' in the Longdendale account for that year (SC 6/802/17, m. 5.) See Table 1, p. xxxviii, and P.I.

59 See **7.10** and **3.08** above.

60 See **7.07**, **7.11** and **5.52**.

m. 3d

reddit alium denarium pro ten(emento) in eadem villa. **3.12** Item
quod Ricardus de Eton',[(u)] qui est [(v)] etatis xv annorum
tenet medietatem Manerij de Hattreslegh' per servicium militare,
per descensum hereditarium,[(w)] et per servicia metendi in autumpno per tres dies,
et in quadragesima [(x)] cum una caruca per iij dies
ad pastum ut supra, et faciendi *Haghehag'*
per iij dies ut supra et opera molendini ut supra.
3.13 Et W(illelmus) de Caryngton, Chivaler, tenet aliam medietatem
per eadem servicia ut supra. Et invenient
unum Judicem in Curia de Mottrum. Et idem
Ricardus et Willelmus reddunt domino per annum pro Reveyeld et Ward' ix d. **3.14** Item quod Johannes de
Hyde, Howel ap Oweyn [(y)]
et filius Willelmi de Tranemol' et
filia Galfridi de Honford tenet[(z)]
in Mottrum in *le Haghe* unum mesuagium et j
carucatam terre per servicium militare, et reddunt per annum iiij s.
3.15 Item, Johannes de Hyde tenet in eadem unum mesuagium
et septem acras terre apud (!)[(a)] per servicium militare et reddit
domino xiij d. per annum.[(b)]
3.16 Item Ricardus de Diewysnape tenet
unum mesuagium et medietatem unius bovate terre et
reddit per annum v s. ij d. [in eadem][(bb)] per annum.
3.17 Item, Radulphus de Wolegh tenet in eadem
j mesuagium et octo acras terre per eadem servicia, et reddit per annum iij s.
3.18 Item, Johannes de Hyde tenet in Mottrum unam placeam
que vocatur *le G[rene]house*[(c)] et dat iij d. pro
Reveyeld et pro Ward' j d.

(u) *tenet* struck through.
(v) *infra etatem* struck through, *etatis xv annorum* interlineated.
(w) *per descensum hereditarium* interlineated.
(x) *cum* struck through.
(y) *Willelmus de Car | yngton* struck through.
(z) *manerium de* struck through after contracted form which usually represents *tenet*; *in* inserted before next line.
(a) *apud* interlineated (and place-name presumably omitted).
(b) *preter sectam sectam* (!) *molendini dicti* next written struck through and cross added.
(bb) *ij d.* interlineated, *in eadem* possibly struck through.
(c) Or *G[reve]house*.

m. 3d

[Hattersley]

3.12   Item that Richard de Eton,[61] who is 15 years of age, holds half the manor of Hattreslegh by knight service, by hereditary descent, and by the services of reaping in harvest time for three days and (ploughing) in Lent with one plough for three days at a meal as above,[62] and of doing haghehag for 3 days as above and works of the mill as above.[63]

3.13   And W(illiam) de Caryngton (Carrington), knight, holds the other half by the same services as above. And they will find one doomsman in the Court of Mottrum.[64] And the same Richard and William render to the lord for reveyeld and ward 9d.

[Mottram]

3.14   Item, that John de Hyde, Howel ap Oweyn and the son of William de Tranemol, and the daughter of Geoffrey de Honford holds (!) in Mottrum in *le Haghe*[65] one messuage and 1 carucate of land by knight service and render yearly 4s.[66]

3.15   Item, John de Hyde holds in the same one messuage and seven acres of land at [...]⁶⁷ by knight service and renders to the lord 13d. yearly.

3.16   Item, Richard de Diewysnape holds one messuage and half of one bovate of land and renders yearly 5s. 2d. yearly.[68]

3.17   Item, Ralph de Wolegh holds in the same 1 messuage and eight acres of land by the same services, and renders yearly 3s.[69]

3.18   Item, John de Hyde holds in Mottrum one place which is called *le G[rene]house*[70] and gives 3d. for reveyeld and for ward 1d.

---

61 See **7.12**. Richard Eton (alias Stokeport), son of Robert Eton (alias Stokeport) and Isabel Davenport (Earwaker, ii. 274). In May 1354 it was found that the Black Prince had no right to the wardship of Richard son of Robert Eton, since he held the manor of Stockport from Sir Hugh Despenser, and the manors of Poynton and Woodford from Geoffrey Poutrell.

62 See **3.05** above and **5.55–56**.

63 See **3.08** above and **5.57** and the extract from the Inquisition Post Mortem of Isabel Stokeport, 1370, given in note 294 below, p. 71.

64 See **7.13** and **5.63**.

65 This has been identified with The Hague in Mottram. See Dodgson, i. 314. This Hague seems likely to be one place where the service of *haghehag'*, first referred to and defined in **3.08**, was performed. See Nevell & Walker, p. 57.

66 See **7.15** and **5.47**. It is perhaps significant that no manor of Mottram is mentioned, and that *the manor of* was crossed out in this entry, but that this is nevertheless the first property listed and apparently the largest. See above, note 55.

67 See **7.16**. The place-name is omitted in both entries. See also **5.50**, and **4.08** from which it appears that this land of John de Hyde was then occupied by Henry Gybon. See above, note 55, and below, note 76.

68 See **7.18**; **5.49**; **4.10**; **3.01**; **6.01** and **7.01**.

69 See **7.19** and **5.48**, where the property is named *le Brodlathum*. See also **3.01** above with note 30.

70 The defective place-name has been supplemented from the parallel entry **7.17**. From **4.09** it appears that this property of John de Hyde was also then occupied by Henry Gybon. See below, note 77.

m. 4

[Very thin, fine parchment (flesh side) 27.5 cm. high × 9.5 cm wide.]

MARTINMAS RENTAL   Both sides of membrane 4 contain a list of rents from parts of the lordship, mainly for half a year, in a different hand from mm. 3, 6 and 7.

4.01	Mottrum de termino Sancti Martini	
4.02	De Stephano de Harap'	ij s.
4.03	De eodem pro terra in *le Haghe*	ii d.
4.04	De Ricardo de Riggeway	vij s.
4.05	De eodem Ricardo pro Ward' et Revegeld	j d. ob.
4.06	De Henrico Gybon'	xviij d.
4.07	De eodem pro Ward' et Revegeld	ii d. ob.
4.08	De eodem pro parte terre Johannis de Hyde	vj d. ob.
4.09	De eodem pro Revegeld	j d. ob.
4.10	De Ricardo de Dewysnape	ij s. vj d.
4.11	De eodem pro Ward' et Revegeld	j d. ob.
4.12	De Jordano del Haghe	ij s. iiij d. ob.
4.13	De eodem pro Ward' et Revegeld	ij d. ob.
4.14	De Willelmo de Godelegh'	iiij s. vij d.
4.15	De eodem pro Ward' et Revegeld	ij d. ob.
4.16	De Adam de Harap'	ij s. j d. ob.
4.17	De Stephano fratre eius	ij s. j d. ob.

m. 4

MARTINMAS RENTAL

4.01	Mottrum (Mottram) from Martinmas Term[71]		
4.02	From Stephen de Harap (Harrop)[72]	2s.	
4.03	From the same for land in *le Haghe*[73]		2d.
4.04	From Richard de Riggeway (Ridgeway)[74]	7s.	
4.05	From the same Richard for ward and revegeld		1½d.
4.06	From Henry Gybon[75]		18d.
4.07	From the same for ward and revegeld		2½d.
4.08	From the same for part of the land of John de Hyde[76]		6½d.
4.09	From the same for revegeld[77]		1½d.
4.10	From Richard de Dewysnape[78]	2s.	6d.
4.11	From the same for ward and revegeld[78a]		1½d.
4.12	From Jordan del Haghe[79]	2s.	4½d.
4.13	From the same for ward and revegeld		2½d.
4.14	From William de Godelegh[80]	4s.	7d.
4.15	From the same for ward and revegeld		2½d.
4.16	From Adam de Harap[81]	2s.	1½d.
4.17	From Stephen his brother[82]	2s.	1½d.

71 For all persons mentioned in this membrane, see P.I. Most of the rents listed here are elucidated in statements made in m. 3, m. 6 or m. 7, and many are also paralleled by entries in m. 5. Attention is drawn to these references in the following notes.

72 This appears to be Stephen de Harap the elder. See **6.52** and **5.29** where the messuage with land adjacent referred to here is called *le Holehous'*. He is named from Harrop Edge, a hill north-west of Mottram. See Dodgson, i. 312.

73 No explanation of this payment has been found in m. 3, m. 6 or m. 7, and this tenancy is likely to be later than those membranes. For *le Haghe* see **3.14** and note 65.

74 This payment and the next appear to relate to the messuage and land adjacent described in **6.58–59** as Hugh del Ruggeway's. See **5.34**. For the place-name see Dodgson, i. 316.

75 For a messuage with land adjacent see **6.50** and **5.30**.

76 This payment appears to be for Sir John Hyde's messuage and seven acres of land at an unspecified place in Mottram: see **3.15**; **7.16**; **5.50** and P.I. This property may have been included among those sold by Sir John Hyde in 1364: see above, note 55, and Introduction. p. xx.

77 This entry seems to imply that Henry Gybon was now also occupying Sir John Hyde's place in Mottram called *le Grenehouse*: see **3.18**, and **7.17**. This and the previous entry may indicate consequences of Sir John Hyde's involvement in the murder of Geoffrey de Honford. See P.I.

78 For a messuage and half a bovate of land see **3.16**, **7.18** and P.I.

78a There is no mention of this ward and revegeld in **3.16** or **7.18**.

79 For a messuage with land adjacent (presumably on the Hague) see **6.51** and **5.32**.

80 This entry and the next appear to refer to the messuage with land adjacent described in **6.55** as held by William son of John. See also **5.20**.

81 For a messuage with land adjacent (possibly at Harrop Edge) see **6.48** and **5.35**.

82 For a messuage with land adjacent (also possibly at Harrop Edge): see **6.49** and **5.35**. This is Stephen de Harap the younger.

m. 4

4.18	De eisdem pro Ward' et Revegeld	ob. qu.
4.19	De Wadkyn del Haghe	iij s. j d. ob.
4.20	De eodem pro Ward' et Revegeld	ij d. ob.
4.21	De Thoma Foucher[d]	xij d.
4.22	De Willelmo de Wharell	xvij d.
4.23	De eodem pro Ward' et Revegeld	j d. ob.
4.24	De Rogero de B(o)thum de Mottrum	ij s.
4.25	**Summa**	xxxiij s. x. d. qu.

4.26	**Tengetwysell**	
4.27	De Willelmo le Mulnere	v s. vj d.
4.28	De Rogero de Bothum pro Arnwayfeld'	xxiij s.
4.29	De eodem pro Ward' et Revegeld	vij d. ob.
4.30	De Willelmo filio suo pro uno burgagio	vj d.
4.31	De Thoma le Barker	iij s. vij d.
4.32	De eodem pro uno burgagio	vj d.
4.33	De Johanne hobrode	iij s. vij d.
4.34	De eodem pro uno burgagio	viij d.
4.35	De Henrico le Wylde pro uno burgagio	x d. ob.
4.36	De eodem pro terra in *Rodefeld'*	iiij s. iij d.
4.37	De Roberto Godard	vj s.

(d) Or *Foncher*.

m. 4

4.18	From them for ward and revegeld		¾d.
4.19	From Wadkyn del Haghe[83]	3s.	1½d.
4.20	From the same for ward and revegeld		2½d.
4.21	From Thomas Foucher[84]		12d.
4.22	From William de Wharell (Warhill)[85]		17d.
4.23	From the same for ward and revegeld		1½d.
4.24	From Roger de Bothum from Mottram[86]	2s.	
4.25	**Sum**	33s.	10¼d.

4.26	**Tengetwysell** (Tintwistle)		
4.27	From William le Mulnere[87]	5s.	6d.
4.28	From Roger de Bothum for Arnwayfeld (Arnfield)[88]	23s.	
4.29	From the same for ward and revegeld		7½d.
4.30	From William his son for one burgage[89]		6d.
4.31	From Thomas le Barker[90]	3s.	7d.
4.32	From the same for one burgage[91]		6d.
4.33	From John Hobrode[92]	3s.	7d.
4.34	From the same for one burgage[93]		8d.
4.35	From Henry le Wylde for one burgage[94]		10½d.
4.36	From the same for land in *Rodefeld*[95]	4s.	3d.
4.37	From Robert Godard[96]	6s.	

83 This appears to be the person referred to in **6.53** as Watkyn Rowessone, holding a messuage with land adjacent (presumably on the Hague), and in **5.33** as Walter Ralph's son. See P.I.

84 This payment is for *Little Rudyng*: see **6.60** with note 255.

85 For a messuage with land adjacent: see **6.54** and **5.31**. Warhill is the hill on which Mottram Church stands. Dodgson, i. 315.

86 For a messuage with land adjacent (perhaps where Botham's Hall is now): see **6.57**.

87 Miller of the mill at Tintwistle, for two messuages with land adjacent: see **6.44** and **5.23**. A certain William le Mulner farmed the mill of Tintwistle, with gaps, up to Michaelmas 1367, when Robert le Smyth took the farm. See Introduction, p. xxviii and below, note 147, p. 35.

88 This payment was half a year's rent for Great and Little Arnfield. See **6.45–46** and **5.22**.

89 This burgage may be the one described in **6.09** as held by his father.

90 In **4.31** and **4.33** Thomas le Barker and John Hobrode appear to be sharing equally the rents arising from the properties referred to in **6.17**, **6.39** and **6.40**, though there now appears to have been an increase of 4d. in their annual rent, perhaps for more land.

91 See **6.14** and **5.09**.

92 See above, note 90.

93 With a certain toft in fee: see **6.34** and **5.10**.

94 Held in fee for the term of his wife's life, with a toft: see **6.27** and **5.08**.

95 With a burgage: see **6.29** and **5.03**. Dodgson, i. 325 suggests that this may be identified with Rhodeswood.

96 This Martinmas term payment of 6s. implies an annual rent of 12s. The only such rent in Tintwistle otherwise unexplained in these membranes is from *Ewodeheye* in **5.21** where no tenant is named, and of this **6.42** says 'is accustomed to render 12s. a year', implying a degree of uncertainty. This property does not, however, appear under 'Decay of Rent' in the 1357–61 accounts: it was productive in both membranes 6 and 5, but it is only here that a tenant is identified. See note 145 below, p. 35.

m. 4

4.38	De Ricardo de Halghton pro burgagiis suis	xxiij d.
4.39	De eodem pro terra sua	iiij s. vj d.
4.40	De Thoma Fabro	iij d.
4.41	De Magota uxore Roberti Dokeson'	ij s. iij d.
4.42	De Roberto Dokeson pro burgagio	iij d.
4.43	De terra Johannis de Hyde	xiiij s. v d.
4.44	De Thoma le Barker	iij d. ob.
4.45	De Willelmo de Thorntelegh'	vij s. iij d.
4.46	De Roberto Dewysnape pro iij burgagiis	ix d. ob.
4.47	De eodem	viij d.
4.48	De Willelmo Geffreu	xij d.
4.49	De Johanne filio Johannis de Dewysnape	v d.
4.50	De Adam de Gaunt[(dd)]	xj s. xj d. ob.

(dd) Or perhaps *Gamit.*

m. 4

4.38	From Richard de Halghton[97] for his burgages		23d.
4.39	From the same for his land[98]	4s.	6d.
4.40	From Thomas the smith[99]		3d.
4.41	From Magot wife of Robert Dokeson[100]	2s.	3d.
4.42	From Robert Dokeson for a burgage[101]		3d.
4.43	From land of John de Hyde[102]	14s.	5d.
4.44	From Thomas le Barker[103]		3½d.
4.45	From William de Thorntelegh[104]	7s.	3d.
4.46	From Robert Dewysnape for 3 burgages[105]		9½d.
4.47	From the same[106]		8d.
4.48	From William Geffreu[107]		12d.
4.49	From John son of John de Dewysnape[108]		5d.
4.50	From Adam de Gaunt[109]	11s.	11½d.

97 Presumably named either from Haughton Green, Lancashire, or Halton, Cheshire. There is no mention of Richard de Halghton's tenure of burgages in m. 6, so these appear to be new tenancies. See **6.38**, Appendix, p. 82 and P.I.

98 This was *le Wallefeld*. See **6.38** and **5.04**.

99 This payment seems likely to relate to the messuage with a certain forge described in **6.28** as held in fee by Henry le Smyth de Stokport: see P.I.

100 Dok's family provide some of the most intriguing puzzles of these manuscripts. See Introduction, p. xxxiii, Appendix, pp. 77f. and P.I. The payment recorded here appears to be a half year's rent paid by her daughter-in-law for the various holdings described in **6.16**; **6.22**; **6.23**; **6.26** and **6.26b** as held by Magot' Dok's wife, with the possible exception of either croft or toft, or with some other adjustment.

101 See **6.24** where the land is described as a toft. See Introduction, p. xxxiii, Appendix, pp. 77f. and P.I.

102 I.e. John son of William de Hyde. This appears to have been a year's, not half-year's, payment for 6 burgages and 9 acres of land: see **6.32** and **5.12**. It may include an element of arrears arising from John de Hyde having been outlawed. See P.I.

103 This otherwise unspecified payment may perhaps relate to the holding referred to in **4.31** above, or possibly to the burgage which had previously been Cobbok's listed in **6.17**, and may not be for the whole period.

104 This payment was a half-year's rent for a burgage and (presumably considerable) lands adjacent. See **6.41** and **5.18**.

105 This payment appears to relate to (a) a burgage: see **6.10** and **5.13**; (b) a toft: see **6.18**; and (c) a parcel of land: see **6.20**.

106 This payment appears to be unexplained elsewhere in these mss, and may indicate a tenancy entered into after m. 6 was made. See Appendix, p. 82 and P.I.

107 See **6.19** which refers to a burgage with land adjacent at an annual rent of 2s. and **5.24** where his rent is 12d. for 1 acre followed by another 12d. in **5.25** for *herstancloghous*.

108 This payment may perhaps relate to the burgage referred to in **5.14**, which does not appear under this name in m. 6. The half-year's rent matches that of the burgage held by John le Tieu in **6.11**. See Appendix, p. 82.

109 This and entries **4.51–52** and **4.54** appear to represent the various persons' Martinmas term shares of the rent due for the jointly held Micklehurst and Littlehurst: see **6.47** and **5.38**. Note that these rents amount to £2 4s. 3⅓d., which would give an annual sum of £4 8s. 7d., an increase on the £4 6s. 8d. of **5.38** and **6.47**, but not as much as the £5 2s. 4d. in the 1366–68 accounts: see Introduction, p. xix, Table 3, p. xl and Appendix, p. 80. Adam de Gaunt is further identified in the Macclesfield Hundred Eyre Indictment Roll (CHES 25/20), m. 24 (1367) as *de Sadilworthfrith* (Saddleworth Forest) further up the Tame valley in Yorkshire.

m. 4

4.51	De Willelmo Symeson	x s. xj d.
4.52	De [Thoma] filio [Ricardi] Capellani	x s. v d. ob.
4.53	[respice in tergo]	

m. 4d

[Written on up-turned membrane, i.e. the other way up from the recto (hair side).]

4.54	De [Simone] Molendinario	x s. xj d. ob.
4.55	**Holynworth**	
4.56	De Roberto de Holynworth	vj d.
4.57	De eodem pro [una] placea iuxta molendinum	j d.
4.58	De R(adulfo) [Ti]llessone	xviij d.
4.59	De eodem [..........]	xij d.
4.60	**Summa**	xlvj s. v d.
4.61	De Ricardo de Wolegh de libero redditu	vj d.
4.62	De eodem Ricardo pro Reveyeld	ob. qu.
4.63	**Summa totalis**	viij li. iij s. iiij d. qu.
4.64	Mattelegh pro Reveyeld	iij d.
4.65	Et pro Warde	j d.

m. 4

4.51	From William Symeson[110]	10s.	11d.
4.52	From [Thomas] son of [Richard] the Chaplain[111]	10s.	5½d.
4.53	[Please turn over.][112]		

m. 4d

4.54	From [Simon] the miller[113]	10s.	11½d.
4.55	**Holynworth** (Hollingworth)		
4.56	From Robert de Holynworth[114]		6d.
4.57	From the same for [one] plot of land next to the mill		1d.
4.58	From R(alph) Tillessone[115]		18d.
4.59	From the same [..........][116]		12d.
4.60	**Sum**	46s.	5d.
4.61	From Richard de Wolegh from free rent[117]		6d.
4.62	From the same Richard for reveyeld[118]		¾d.
4.63	**Sum total** £8	3s.	4¼d.
4.64	Mattelegh (Matley) for reveyeld[119]		3d.
4.65	And for ward		1d.

110 It seems likely that Symeson is the patronymic of William del Fernylegh. See **6.47**, **5.38** and P.I.
111 Alias Thomas le Prestessone: see **6.47**.
112 The group of Micklehurst and Littlehurst rents continues overleaf though without any reference to John Lastles, presumably again reflecting a situation later than that in m. 6.
113 See **4.50** above, with note 109, and **6.47**, where he is called *le Muleward*. The scribe of this membrane (or his exemplar) sometimes prefers Latin expression, cf. **4.40** and **4.52** above.
114 One of the jurors who made the Extent: see **3.01**, **6.01**, **7.01**. No explanation of this payment or the next appears elsewhere in the mss. It may perhaps represent a half year's rent either from *Oldefeld*, **6.07**, **7.26**, **5.59**, or possibly from one of the two plots of meadow land in Woolley mentioned in the 1359–60 accounts under 'Increase of Rent'. See Appendix, p. 82 and Table 1 with notes, pp. xxxviii, xli–xlii.
115 Cf. **6.56** where the name is spelt *Tyllessone*. The property to which this rent relates is not identified, but the payment would be appropriate for Ralph de Wolegh, who held *le Brodlathum* in Mottram for 3s. a year: see **3.17**, **7.19** and **5.48**. The possibility must be considered that Tillessone was Ralph de Wolegh's patronymic.
116 This payment presumably relates to the *Thomerode* of **6.56**, though that also is listed under Mottram. See note 252 there.
117 For a third part of Little Hollingworth: see **6.05**, **7.24** and **5.46**.
118 See **6.05**.
119 For this entry and the next see **2.05** and **3.06**: these are whole year's payments. The fact that the place rather than the person is named accords with the doubt expressed in **3.06** about Sir John de Hyde's right to hold the manor.

m. 4d

4.66	De Terra Johannis de Hyde	xx d.
4.67	De terra Willelmi de Mattelegh	ij s. iiij d.
4.68	De Johanne de Hyde pro terra de Warde	
	filij Roberti de Holynworth'	vj s.
4.69	De Roberto de Deuwesnape de redditu	iiij s.
4.70	De Cristiana de Holynworth' de redditu	xviij d.
4.71	De Willelmo filio eius	j d. ob.
4.72	De reveyeld'	iiij d. ob.
4.73	**Summa**	xvj s. iiij d.

m. 4d

4.66	From the land of John De Hyde[120]		20d.
4.67	From the land of William de Mattelegh[121]	2s.	4d.
4.68	From John de Hyde for the land of the wardship of the son of Robert de Holynworth[122]	6s.	
4.69	From Robert de Deuwesnape from rent[123]	4s.	
4.70	From Christiana de Holynworth from rent[124]		18d.
4.71	From William her son[125]		1½d.
4.72	From reveyeld		4½d.
4.73	**Sum**	16s.	4d.

120 It is not clear to which of John de Hyde's holdings this payment relates: see the next note, P.I. and **4.08**.
121 This name, not found elsewhere in these mss, may refer to the William de Hyde who died seised of half the manor of Matley: see **3.06**. The combined rents of this and the previous entry would amount to the 4s. due annually as the free rent of Matley: see **3.08**, **5.51**, Tables 1 and 3, pp. xxxviii, xl and Appendix, p. 73.
122 See **3.08** and **7.06**, where Henry son of Robert de Hollingworth is described as holding a fourth part of the manor of Matley, by the service of 4s. from the whole manor, *haghehag* and earth-work at Tintwistle mill, etc. He is not there called a ward, but the situation is revealed by the 1359–60 Accounts (SC 6/802/17, m. 5) which record for the first time the receipt of 6s. for the custody of the lands and tenements of Henry son and heir of Alice daughter of William de Matley, under age, viz. 14 that year, for a fourth part of the township of Matley. The follow-ing account (SC 6/803/3, m. 5) from Michaelmas 1360 to Lady Day 1361, when the lordship was farmed to Sir William Caryngton, notes receipt of the half-year's 3s. That half-year includ-ed Martinmas 1360. This Martinmas entry, like some others above, presents a whole year's receipt and must thus be later than Lady Day 1361. See Introduction, p. xix. Henry was still in wardship in 1366–68 (SC 6/803/13, mm. 3, 4).
123 For a burgage with land adjacent called *Aspenforlong*: see **6.35** and **5.19**.
124 For two-thirds of Little Hollingworth and Thorncliffe: see **6.06**, **7.25** and **5.45**. Since it is not clear how this lady would have been named in English, whether *Christine* or *Christiana*, we have used the name written in the original: **6.07b** has *Cristiana* unabbreviated.
125 This William is not so named elsewhere in these mss. It may be, however, that the William in question is otherwise known as William de Thorntelegh. The reasons for this payment and the next are not explained, though they amount to a half year's revegeld due from Christiana.

m. 5

[Paper(d*)   29.5 cm. high × 13.5–14.0 cm wide.]

*Both sides of m. 5 contain an explicitly-titled extent in rental form, apparently showing expected yearly receipts, in the same hand as **m. 4**.*

5.01	**Extenta de Longeden'**	
5.02	**Teng'**	**Termini Sancti Martini et Pentecostes**
5.03	De Henrico le Wyld(e) *Rodefeld*	viij s. vj d.(f) ad festa Sancti Martini et Pentecostes
5.04	De Ricardo de Halghton pro *le Wallefeld* ad eosdem terminos	ix s.
5.05	De Mag' filia Doke de redditu ad eosdem terminos	ij s.
5.06	De Nicholao filio Willelmi ad eosdem terminos pro burg(agiis)	iij s. x d.
5.07	De Mag' filia Doke pro Burgagio	xij d.
5.08	De Henrico le Wylde pro burgagio	xij d.
5.09	De Thoma le Barker(g)	xij d.
5.10	De Johanne Hobrod pro burg'	xvj d.
5.11	De Willelmo le Hune(h) pro burg'(i)	xvj d.
5.12	De Johanne de Hyde pro burgagiis	xiiij s. v d. levab'(j)

(d*) This leaf displays a large, clear watermark.
(e) *Henrico le Wyld* interlineated.
(f) *vj d.* interlineated.
(g) *pro burg'* next written struck through.
(h) Or perhaps *Hund'*.
(i) In this and the previous entry *burg'* may represent either *burgagio* or perhaps more likely *burgagiis*. See notes 134 and 135 opposite.
(j) Presumably *levabitur* or *levabilis*, though *levabatur* is also possible.

m. 5

5.01	**Extent of Longeden(dale)**	
5.02	**Teng'** (Tintwistle)	**Martinmas and Pentecost Terms**[126]
5.03	From Henry le Wyld[127] *Rodefeld*	8s. 6d. at the feasts of St Martin and Pentecost
5.04	From Richard de Halghton for *le Wallefeld*[128] at the same terms	9s.
5.05	From Mag' Dok's daughter from rent at the same terms[129]	2s.
5.06	From Nicholas son of William at the same terms for burgages[130]	3s. 10d.
5.07	From Mag' Dok's daughter for a burgage[131]	12d.
5.08	From Henry le Wylde for a burgage[132]	12d.
5.09	From Thomas le Barker[133]	12d.
5.10	From John Hobrod for burgage(s)[134]	16d.
5.11	From William le Hune' (*or* Hund')[135] for burgage(s)	16d.
5.12	From John de Hyde for burgages[136]	14s. 5d. (will be) levied

126 For all persons named in this membrane see P.I. Most of the receipts listed are elucidated by statements in m. 3, m. 6 or m. 7, and many are paralleled by rents in m. 4. Attention is drawn to these references in the following notes.

127 See **6.29** and **4.36**.

128 See **6.38** and **4.39**. The place-name may mean 'the spring field' (Dodgson, i. 328).

129 This rent appears to be for the three burgages held at will by Magot Dok's wife in **6.16**: see also **4.41**, note 100 and Introduction, p. xxxiii.

130 This rent from Nicholas son of William son of Thomas (Dykeson) was for two burgages, three tofts and one croft with appurtenances. See **6.21b**, **6.25** and P.I.

131 See **6.26**, where the burgage is described as held by Magot Dok's wife. See Introduction, p. xxxiii.

132 This entry may relate to the burgage with a toft which Henry le Wylde held for the term of his wife's life. See **6.27** where the rent is given as 21d. a year. Since 12d. was the normal rent of a burgage, this may imply that he no longer held the toft.

133 I.e. bark-stripper or tanner. The rent may be for either of the burgages referred to in **6.14** and **6.17**, though the former may be more likely.

134 This rent is for a burgage with a certain toft. See **6.34** and **4.34**.

135 This is the only reference to this William by this name in these mss. The only William among the Tintwistle tenants listed in m. 6 whose holding is not clearly identified in mm. 4 and 5 is William Nyksone in **6.12–13**, whose grange with curtilage and toft together yield 6d. yearly. Also, in **4.30** William son of Roger de Bothum pays 6d. Martinmas term rent for one burgage, presumably that held by his father in **6.09**. Either of these might be the person referred to here. The *burg'* in this entry may be singular or plural, and the 16d. may indicate that either tenant had now taken more land or this may be a new tenant.

136 This entry relates to six burgages and nine acres of land held by John son of William de Hyde. See **6.32** and **4.43**. The note *levab'* may mean 'used to be levied' but 'will be levied' or 'leviable' are perhaps more likely in view of the fact that this John had been outlawed. See P.I.

m. 5

5.13	De Roberto de Dewsnape pro burgagio	xij d.
5.14	De Johanne⁽ʲʲ⁾ filio Johann(is) de Dewsnape pro eodem	xij d.
5.15	De Roberto le Smyth pro eodem	xij d.
5.16	De burgagio quod fuit Roberti le Smyth senioris	vij d.
5.17	De fabrica Symonis fabri	vij d.
5.18	⁽ᵏ⁾De Willelmo de Thorntelegh'	xiiij s. iij d.
5.19	De Roberto de Dewsnape pro *aspenforlong*	viij s.
5.20	De terra Johannis de Godelegh'	xj s. iiij d.
5.21	De *Ewodeheye*	xij s.
5.22	De Rogero de Bothum pro *Arnewayfeld'*	xlvj s.
5.23	De Willelmo le Mulner	xj s.

(jj) *Johanne* interlineated.
(k) A note in the left-hand margin against this entry reads *Ten(ens) ad voluntatem.*

m. 5

5.13	From Robert de Dewsnape for a burgage[137]	12d.
5.14	From John son of John de Dewsnape[138] for the same	12d.
5.15	From Robert le Smyth[139] for the same	12d.
5.16	From the burgage that was Robert le Smyth the elder's[140]	7d.
5.17	From the forge of Symon the smith[141]	7d.
5.18	From William de Thorntelegh[142]	14s. 3d.
5.19	From Robert de Dewsnape for *aspenforlong*[143]	8s.
5.20	From the land of John de Godelegh[144]	11s. 4d.
5.21	From *Ewodeheye*[145]	12s.
5.22	From Roger de Bothum for *Arnewayfeld*[146] (Arnfield)	46s.
5.23	From William le Mulner[147]	11s.

137 See **6.10** and P.I.
138 John son of John de Dewsnape is referred to also in **4.49**, but apparently not in m. 6: see next note.
139 This Robert is referred to only here in these mss. Entries **6.36–37** below refer to burgages 'in decay' with rents of 12d. The accounts for the period 1357–61 indicate changes in the lands 'in decay', in particular the burgage that had been William le Stiwardesson's (**6.37**), mentioned under that heading in the accounts from the Escheator's of 1357–58 as far as Tieu's to Michaelmas 1359 (SC 6/802/15, m. 1) disappears after that date and may be referred to here. This and the previous entry may reveal the filling of vacant burgages subsequent to the taking of the jury's evidence on Tintwistle given in m. 6. A certain Robert le Smyth of Stayley, who may be the same person, took the mill of Tintwistle at farm for a term of six years at a yearly rent of 30s. from Michaelmas 1367 (SC 6/803/13, m 4.)
140 See **6.30**, where this holding is described as 'one messuage upon (*or* above) *le Syk*'.
141 This entry refers to the 'plot with curtilage which was Symon le Smyth's, in decay' which formerly rendered 9d. See **6.31**. The decay of rent of 9d. from this property, formerly Faber's (le Smyth's), was first listed in Tieu's 1359–60 account (SC 6/802/17, m. 5) and continued as the half-year's 4½d. in his next and last of Michaelmas 1360 to 26 March 1361 (SC 6/803/3, m. 5). This entry with its 7d. rent must therefore postdate that account, and this membrane must date from Sir William Caryngton's time as farmer of the lordship. See Introduction, p. xx.
142 For a burgage with (considerable) lands adjacent: see **6.41** and **4.45**. The annual rent was 14s. 6d., and it is possible that the discrepancy here may be the result of a simple scribal error (*iij d.* for *vj d.*). A note in the margin reads 'Tenant at will'.
143 This rent was for a burgage with land adjacent: see **6.35** and **4.69**. The place-name appears to relate to a field or group of fields so far unidentified. In the 1408 Rental of Longdendale (MS. Harl. 2039, f. 113) a Roger Scott paid 2s. 6¼d. as a tenant at will for *le aspinforlonge*.
144 There is no record in m. 6 or m. 7 of a substantial holding in Tintwistle by any person of this name, nor has the rent been precisely identified elsewhere, though the reference may be to the messuage with land adjacent listed in **6.55** as held by William son of John for a yearly rent of 9s. 6d. including revegeld and ward 4d., though that is included amongst Mottram holdings. See also **4.14–15** and Appendix, p. 76.
145 See **6.42**, which states that *le Heewodeheyghe* is accustomed to render 12s., no tenant being named. In **4.37** a Robert Godard paid a Martinmas term rent of 6s., which appears to refer to this land. Dodgson, i. 327 refers to the modern field-name How Day Head Meadow in Tintwistle, and interprets the name as '(enclosure at) a wood by a river'.
146 This was a year's rent for Great and Little Arnfield not including revegald and ward. See **6.45–46** and **4.28**.
147 For two messuages with land adjacent: see **6.44** and **4.27** with note 87.

m. 5

5.24	De Willelmo Geffreu pro j acra	xij d.
5.25	De eodem pro *herstancloghous'*	xij d.
5.26	De *[Rest of line blank.]*	
5.27	**Summa**	vij li. xj s. viij d.[(l)]
5.28	**Mottrum**	**Ad eosdem terminos**
5.29	De Stephano de Harap' pro *le holehous'*	iiij s.
5.30	De Henrico Gybon'	iij s.
5.31	De Willelmo del Wharell'	vij s.
5.32	De Jordano del Hagh'	iiij s. ix d.
5.33	De Waltero filio Radulfi	vij s.
5.34	De Ricardo de Ruggeway	xiiij s.
5.35	De Stephano et Adam de Harap'	vij s.
5.36	De Adam le Tayllour	x s. j d. in decasu
5.37	**Summa**	lvj s. x d.[(m)]

(l) In the right-hand margin *vij li. xj s. viij d.* struck through.
(m) In the right-hand margin *lxxj s. x d.* struck through.

m. 5

5.24	From William Geffreu[148] for 1 acre		12d.
5.25	From the same for *herstancloghous*[149]		12d.
5.26	From [*Rest of line blank.*]		
5.27		**Sum** £7	11s.	8d.[150]

5.28	**Mottrum** (Mottram)	**At the same terms**	
5.29	From Stephen de Harap for *le holehous*'[151]	4s.	
5.30	From Henry Gybon[152]	3s.	
5.31	From William del Wharell[153]	7s.	
5.32	From Jordan del Hagh[154]	4s.	9d.
5.33	From Walter son of Ralph[155]	7s.	
5.34	From Richard de Ruggeway[156]	14s.	
5.35	From Stephen and Adam de Harap[157]	7s.	
5.36	From Adam le Tayllour[158]	10s.	1d. in decay
5.37	**Sum**	56s.	10d.

148 See **6.19**, where William Geffrou holds in fee 1 burgage with land adjacent for 2s. yearly, and **4.48** which records an unspecified Martinmas rent of 12d. Perhaps this 1 acre was only part of that 'land adjacent'. See also **3.01** with note 34.

149 See **6.21**, where *le Herstoncloghouses* with 6 acres of land adjacent used to render 4s., but lies in decay. Throughout the Longdendale accounts from 1357 until Sir William Caryngton's lease of the lordship in 1361 a 4s. annual rent, regularly identified as due from 'the Herstonclouhouses of Tintwistle', was 'in decay' (the money could not be levied) because the lands were unploughed for lack of tenants. (SC 6/802/15, m. 1; 6/802/17, m. 5; 6/803/3, m. 5.) In that context this entry appears to indicate that William Geffrou was now occupying it at a reduced rent or part of it only, perhaps instead of part of his other property. This tenancy clearly postdated the accounts up to 26 March 1361. Dodgson, i. 328 explains the name as meaning 'houses at the valley where hearth-stones are got'.

150 The total should read £7 12s. 2d. The inaccurate total here coincides with the rent from the 'ter-mors' of Tintwistle in the 1366–68 accounts (SC 6/803/13, mm. 3, 4): see Table 3, p. xl.

151 See **6.52**, where he is identified as 'the elder', and **4.02** with note 72. *Holehous*': 'House in a hollow', Dodgson, i. 316.

152 For a messuage with land adjacent: see **6.50** and **4.06**.

153 See **6.54** and **4.22–23**. The annual rent for his messuage with land adjacent is given in **6.54** as 2s. 10d. + 2½d., figures supported by **4.22**. The 7s. mentioned here is unexplained in these mem-branes, and may perhaps indicate that he now occupied more land.

154 For a messuage with land adjacent: see **6.51** and **4.12–13**.

155 This appears to be Watkyn Rowessone, who in **6.53** held at will 1 messuage with land adja-cent for 6s. 3d. + 4d., and who was almost certainly the same person as Wadkyn del Haghe, who in **4.19–20** paid Martinmas rent of 3s. 1½d. The 7s. here may indicate that he also now occupied more land. Note the striking threefold variation in his name.

156 See **4.04–05**. This payment appears to relate to the messuage with land adjacent described in **6.58–59** as Hugh del Ruggeway's.

157 According to **6.48–49** Adam and Stephen de Harop the younger (named as brothers in **4.16–17**) held at will two messuages with land adjacent for a combined sum of 8s. 6d. + 1¼d., rents reflected almost exactly in the Martinmas 4s. 3d. + ¾d. of **4.16–18**. The 7s. here may therefore indicate that they now occupied less land.

158 This is the only reference to Adam le Tayllour; no parallel has been found elsewhere in these mss for the large Mottram rent here 'in decay'; and no such sum is listed under 'Decay of Rent'.

m. 5

5.38	De tenentibus de Mukklehurst et Littelhurst	iiij li. vj s. viij d.
5.39	De tenentibus de Longedend[..... hun...] pro herbagio	}
5.40	redd' terris arrabil' p[...]nag[....bus] profic'	xij li.

5.41   De molendin(o) ibidem [........] domini r[(e)d....] mercat[.....] cum
Stallagio[(n)]   iiij li.

5.42   **Summa**   xx li. vj s. viij d.[(o)]

m. 5d   [The same way up as the recto.]

5.43   Liberi tenentes ibidem in Longedene Dale

5.44	De Johanne de Holynworth ad eosdem terminos	iij s. iiij d.
5.45	De Cristiana de Holynworth	iij s.
5.46	De Ricardo de Wolegh'	xij d.

(n)   The lower part of m. 5 is in very poor condition, and even under ultra-violet light **5.39–41** are
      only partly intelligible.
(o)   In the right-hand margin *xx li. vj s. viij d.*

m. 5

5.38	From the tenants of Mukklehurst and Littelhurst[159]	£4	6s.	8d.
5.39	From the tenants of Longedend(ale) [........][160]			
	for pasturage	£12[161]		
5.40	(rent) from arable lands [......] profit			
5.41	From the lord's mill there [...] (market) with Stallage[162]	£4		
5.42	**Sum**	£20	6s.	8d.

m. 5d

5.43	**Free tenants there in Longedene Dale**[163]		
5.44	From John de Holynworth[164] at the same terms	3s.	4d.
5.45	From Christiana de Holynworth[165]	3s.	
5.46	From Richard de Wolegh[166]		12d.

in the Longdendale accounts from 1357 to 1361, or from 1366 to 1368. The Mottram properties held at will listed in **6.56**, **6.57**, and **6.60** with annual rents of 2s., 4s. and 2s. respectively are otherwise unaccounted for in this membrane, as indeed are those of free tenants listed in **3.18**, **6.02** and **6.03** with annual rents of 4d., reveyeld and ward, 1¼d., and 1s. 6d. + 1 lb. of cumin repectively. (See Appendix, pp. 75ff.) The 1359–60 account (SC 6/802/17, m. 5) includes under 'Increase of Rent' a new tenement in Mottram called *Prestefeld* with an annual rent of 5s. It is unclear for which lands this tenant might have been paying this 10s. 1d. rent before it fell into decay, but it must be presumed that his tenancy had begun after the Martinmas of m. 4.

159 See **6.47**, where the tenants were named as John Lastles, Simon le Muleward, William del Fernylegh, Adam de Gaunt and Thomas le Prestessone. See also **4.50–54**, where the first is omitted and some of them are named differently, and where the half-yearly rent had increased to £2 4s. 1½d. By the 1366–67 account (SC 6/803/13, m. 3) this annual rent had again increased further to 102s. 4d. Micklehurst, now part of Tameside Metropolitan Borough, was in Tintwistle township, though it is in the Tame valley, as the Littlehurst, now lost, also seems likely to have been. See Earwaker, ii. 173–4, and Dodgson, i. 322.

160 The lacunae in the text of **5.39–41** prevent complete interpretation, though the accounts refer to herbage or agistment.

161 See **2.10** above, with note 12, and **6.63–64** below, with notes 259–60. By 1366 this rent had increased to £13 6s. 8d.: see Table 3, p. xl.

162 What seems to be a defective reference to a market is most tantalising. Stallage is a payment for the right to set up a stall for the purpose of selling goods. See **2.11** above with note 13. The Longdendale accounts for 1357–61 (SC 6/802/15, m. 1, 6/802/17, m. 5, 6/803/3, m. 5) usually mention the farm of the mill and stallage at a fixed rent of £3 yearly, though by 1366–68 that situation had deteriorated, and each relevant account usually lists the issues of the St Bartholomew's Day fair of that year, which in fact varied from 5s. 6½d. to 13s. 4d. See Tables, pp. xxxviii–xl.

163 A number of the figures in this list may be compared with those in m. 2, above.

164 For Great Hollingworth: see **6.04** and **7.23**. The absence of any comparable Martinmas rent in m. 4 is noteworthy.

165 For two-thirds of Little Hollingworth and Thorncliffe: see **6.06**, **7.25** and **4.70**.

166 For one-third of Little Hollingworth: see **6.05**, **7.24** and **4.61–62**.

m. 5d

5.47	De terra Willelmi de Bagylegh in *le Haghe*	iiij s.
5.48	De Radulfo de Wolegh' pro *le Brodlathum*	iij s.
5.49	De Ricardo de Dewsnape	v s. ij d.
5.50	De Johanne de Hyde pro terra in Mottrum	xiij d.
5.51	De Mattelegh'	iiij s.
5.52	De Godelegh'	ij d.
5.53	De Stavelegh' pro diversis redditibus et operibus	xiij s. j d.
5.54	De Neuton' pro arrura et ^(p) *sher[re]ing'*	xj s. j d.
5.55	De Hattreslegh pro arrura	ij s.
5.56	De eadem pro *sheryng'*	vj d.
5.57	De eadem pro *haghagh'*	vj d.

(p) *me* first written struck through.

m. 5d

5.47	From the land of William de Bagylegh[167] in *le Haghe*	4s.	
5.48	From Ralph de Wolegh for *le Brodlathum*[168]	3s.	
5.49	From Richard de Dewsnape[169]	5s.	2d.
5.50	From John de Hyde for land in Mottrum[170]		13d.
5.51	From Mattelegh[171]	4s.	
5.52	From Godelegh[172]		2d.
5.53	From Stavelegh for various rents and works[173]	13s.	1d.
5.54	From Neuton for ploughing and reaping[174]	11s.	1d.
5.55	From Hattreslegh for ploughing[175]	2s.	
5.56	From the same for reaping[176]		6d.
5.57	From the same for haghagh[177]		6d.

167 Presumably William de Baggilegh the younger, who was son of William Baggilegh, knight, of Baguley near Northenden. He became lord of the manor of Godley after 1319, and held it until his death, when the Baggilegh estates seem to have been divided between his two sisters, one of whom was married to John Hyde. It is not clear exactly what happened to the Baguley estates about this period. See Earwaker, ii. 156–7. This land in *le Haghe* may, however, be that referred to in **3.14** and **7.15** as held jointly by Sir John de Hyde, Howel ap Oweyn, the son and heir of William de Tranemol and the daughter and heiress of Geoffrey de Honford, which yielded 4s. a year.

168 One messuage and eight acres of land, presumably at Broadbottom: see **3.17** and **7.19**.

169 For a messuage and half a bovate of land in Mottram: see **3.16**, **7.18** and **4.10–11**.

170 For one messuage and seven acres of land: see **3.15**, **7.16**, and **4.08** from which it appears that this land was then in the occupation of Henry Gybon. See P.I. This property may have been included among those sold by Sir John Hyde in 1364: see above, note 55, p. 19.

171 In the Longdendale account for 1359–60 (SC 6/802/17, m 5) the free rent of Great and Little Matley is given as 4s. See also Introduction, p. xxv and Tables 1 and 2, pp. xxxviii–ix with notes, and **3.08** (and **7.06**), where Henry son of Robert de Holynworth pays 'the service of 4s. for the whole manor'.

172 This sum represents 1d. each from Sir John de Hyde, for half the manor, and from John son of John de Godlegh, for a messuage and 24 acres of land. See **3.10–11**, **7.07** and **7.11**. Cf. Table 1, p. xxxviii.

173 Both **3.04** and **7.27** state that Robert de Stavelegh holds the manor of Stayley from the lord of Longdendale by knight service and that he has been given notice to show by what (additional) services he holds the manor. Whatever those services may have been, this entry and the accounts indicate that they had been commuted for cash payment. At the end of John le Tieu's 1359–60 account (SC 6/802/17, m. 5) there appear two 'Respites' of the rent, works and other services of Robert de Stavelegh because he has shown a relaxation of Robert Holand: 13s. 1d. (for the current year) and 6s. 6½d. (presumably for the previous half year). In the previous accounts, however, the works due from Stayley had been shown at 9s. 9d., as they were again in 1366–68. See Tables 1 and 3, pp. xxxviii, xl. This entry is thus likely to postdate the audit of the 1359–60 accounts.

174 In the 1357–60 accounts (See Table 1, p. xxxviii) the township of Newton is charged 11s. 1d. for ploughing and reaping works due from the lord of Newton and his tenants to the lord of Longdendale. See also **3.05** (and **7.03**, defective) for the very specific conditions on which Newton was held. Note that the scribe started to write a Latin word for reaping (*messione* or a variant), but being unsure of it wrote in English instead.

175 Evidently the cash commutation value of the 'ploughing with one plough for three days' of **3.12** and **7.12**.

176 Similarly the commutation figure for 'reaping for three days' of **3.12** and **7.12**.

177 Similarly the commutation figure for the very interesting service of *haghehag*': see **3.08**, where this

m. 6

6.10   Et quod Robertus de Dewysnape tenet | [18] j Burgagium et reddit per annum ad eosdem terminos xij d.

6.11   Et quod Johannes le Tieu tenet unum [(c)] burgagium et reddit domino per annum ad eosdem terminos x d.

6.12   [(d)] Et quod Willelmus | [19] Nykson tenet unam grangiam et unum curtilagium et reddit domino per annum iiij d.[(e)]

6.13   Et quod idem Willelmus tenet unum toftum et reddit per annum ij d.

6.14   Et quod Thomas | [20] le Barker tenet unum burgagium et reddit per annum ad eosdem terminos xij d.

6.15   Et quod [(f)] Johannes filius Thome le Forster tenet unam parvam domum super | [21] *le Syk'* et reddit per annum vj d.

6.16   Et quod Magota uxor Doke tenet ad voluntatem tria burgagia et reddit per annum ad eosdem terminos ij s.

6.17   Et quod Thomas le Barker tenet | [22] unum burgagium quod fuit Cobbok' ad voluntatem et reddit domino per annum xij d.

6.18   Item, Robertus de Dewysnape tenet unum toftum in feodo et reddit per annum iiij d.

6.19   Item, | [23] Willelmus Geffrou tenet j [(g)] burgagium cum terra adiacenti in feodo et reddit domino per annum ij s.

6.20   Item, Robertus de Dewysnape tenet unam parcellam terre in feodo | [24] et reddit domino per annum iij d.

(c)   *burg'* first written struck through, *acram* interlineated, struck through, *burg'* interlineated.
(d)   *Item Johannes* struck through.
(e)   *vj d.* struck through, *iiij d.* interlineated.
(f)   *Robertus Dokesso* first written struck through.
(g)   *me* struck through.

m. 5d

5.58 De diversis tenentibus in toto dominio de Revegald'[(pp)] x s.
5.59 Del *Oldefeld'* in holynworth'   xij d.

5.60 **Perquisita Cur(iarum)**   xx s.

5.61   iiij li. ij s. xj d.

5.62   **Summa Totalis** xxxv li. vij s. [.j d.]

5.63 **Nomina judicatorum**
    In Mattelegh'   ij   *[Right-hand side*
    In Holynworth'   iij   *of page*
    In Stavelegh'   j   *left blank.]*
    In Hattreslegh'   j

(pp) *de Revegald'* interlineated.

m. 5d

5.58	From various tenants in the whole lordship for revegald[178]		10s.	
5.59	From the *Oldefeld*[179] in Holynworth			12d.
5.60	**Perquisites of the Courts**[180]		20s.	
5.61		£4	2s.	11d.
5.62	**Sum Total**[181]	£35	7s.	[.1d.]

5.63 **Names of doomsmen**[182]

In Mattelegh	2
In Holynworth	3
In Stavelegh	1
In Hattreslegh	1

service is defined, and notes 53 and 294. In **3.12** and **7.12** Richard de Eton is said to hold half the manor of Hattersley by the three services listed here among others. The figures in this and the previous two entries amount to 3s. only, whereas the 1357–60 accounts, which included another 3 services due from Sir William Caryngton (**3.13** and **7.13**) show 3s. 6d. See Table 1, p. xxxviii.

178 See the interlineations in the right-hand column of m. 2 above, with notes *ad. loc.*, and **3.06** with note 50, etc. In the 1357 and 1360 accounts the figure was 13s. 3½d., but in 1358 and 1359 13s. 4d. See Table 1, p. xxxviii.

179 This was a capital messuage in Hollingworth, later held by the Bretland family of Thorncliffe: Earwaker, ii. 146. In **6.07** and **7.26** Philip de Eggerton holds 40 acres of land there (Hollingworth) and renders 12d. These references appear to be to the same holding. See also Dodgson, i. 312. In the 1408 Rental of Longdendale (MS Harl. 2039, f.113) *Ly oldfeld* in Hollingworth rendered only 6¼d.

180 See **2.13** and note 15. From the accounts this appears to be a reasonable round figure.

181 The clerk's totals amount to £34 17s. 11d. Note that the numeral *x* is lacking in the bracket at the line-end, where there is a tear in the paper. This total may be compared with the total of the summary valuation in **2.14**, but does not tally with the 1357–60 accounts. See Table 1, p. xxxviii.

182 Presumably the clerk intended to supply the names of the doomsmen in this list, since the right-hand side of the membrane is left blank. Note that Henry son of Robert de Hollingworth is to find two doomsmen for Matley: see **3.08** and **7.06**; John de Hollingworth is to find one doomsman according to **6.04**, but two according to **7.23**; Richard de Wolley, also of Hollingworth, another one: see **6.05** and **7.24**; and Richard de Eton and Sir William Caryngton together one doomsman for Hattersley: see **3.13** and **7.13**. All these apply to the court at Mottram. In both **3.04** and **7.27** Stayley's services remain to be shown, though this entry implies that finding one doomsman was one of them.

m. 5d

5.64

De bladis Ricardi de Byrche	[......]
De debitis ipsius	[......]
De debitis ipsius in Hyde	[......]
De debitis ipsius de molendino.	[......]

5.65   **L[ong]dendale**(q)

(q) At the bottom of the membrane in a much larger, later hand.

m. 5d

5.64

    From the corn of Richard de Byrche[183]   [......]
    From his debts   [......]
    From his debts in Hyde   [......]
    From his debts from the mill   [......]

5.65   **Longdendale**

183 This section refers to a person who apparently owed money to the lord for some reason. Richard de Byrche does not appear elsewhere in these mss. A Richard Byrches was fined in Shareshull's sessions (1353), of which 26s. 8d. was payable to the poker of Macclesfield in 1354–55 (SC 6/802/11, m. 2), and it is possible that these entries relate to that fine. In the Longdendale accounts for Michaelmas 1357 to 13 September 1358 (SC 6/802/15, m. 1) the herbage, focage and arable of Longdendale were farmed by the steward to Richard del Byrches, Henry Erneshagh and others for £12, but in the following accounts his name does not appear in that capacity. In the 1366–67 account (SC 6/803/13, m. 3) he is named as 'deputy of the same Adam (de Kyngeslegh, then bailiff) in the lordship' exercising responsibility for the sale of the issues of the mill wholesale (*in grosso*) and also as 'keeper of the lord's wood there' with wages of £1 10s. 5d. In the 1367–68 account (SC 6/803/13, m. 4) the keeper of the wood (unnamed) received £1. See P.I. In view of the references to corn and the mill it is also possible that this section might relate to and postdate his role in 1367, though it is clearly a postscript added after the main body of the extent.

m. 6

[Parchment (flesh side) 22.5 cm. high × c. 26 cm. wide.]

PARTLY CANCELLED DRAFT OF THE 1360 EXTENT
Both sides of m. 6 contain parts of what appears to have been a neater draft of
the Extent, mainly cancelled by a line drawn vertically through it from line 16
onwards. Since lines on this membrane are much longer than printed lines, each
new entry is started on a new line and line divisions are shown by | and lines num-
bered.

[1] **6.01** Extenta dominij de Longedale facta die Martis proxime post festum
Conversionis[(r)] Sancti Pauli Apostoli anno regni regis Edwardi tercij a conquestu
tricesimo quarto, | [2] coram Johanne de Delves, Locum tenente Justiciarij Cestrie,
et Magistro Johanne de Brunham Juniore, Camerario Cestrie, per preceptum domi-
ni | [3] Comitis Cestrie ad hoc assignatis, Per sacramentum Roberti de Staveley,
Roberti de Neuton', Ricardi de Woley, [Willelmi] | [4] Gibonsone, Ricardi de
Dewisnape, Roberti de Holynworth, Rogeri del Bothum, Willelmi Geffrou,
Willelmi de Thron | [5] telegh,[(s)] Johannis Lastles, Willelmi del Fernylegh' et
Johannis Hobrode, Juratorum, qui dicunt super sacramentum suum quod.[(t)]
6.02 Item, dicunt quod | [6] Johannes filius Johannis de Radeclyft tenet in Mottrum
unum [(u)] mesuagium cum uno gardino et unam dimidiam rodam terre per (!) et
reddit per annum j d. qu.
6.03 Item, | [7] Willelmus de Caryngton' tenet [(v)] unam placeam vocatam Harop'
in eadem villa per servicium militare et reddit per annum | [8] xviij d. et j lb. Cumin'.

(r) *Conversionis* inserted above line.
(s) Here the name is written in full.
(t) A sign like a large slanted # is inserted here.
(u) *cotagium et una* first written struck through, then *mesuagium cum uno gardino et* interlineated.
(v) *in Harop' in ead* struck through.

m. 6

PARTLY CANCELLED DRAFT OF THE 1360 EXTENT [184]

6.01   Extent of the lordship of Longedale made on Tuesday next after the feast of the Conversion of Saint Paul the Apostle in the thirty-fourth year of the reign of King Edward the third from the conquest, [185] before John de Delves, lieutenant of the Justiciar of Chester, and Master John de Brunham the younger, Chamberlain of Chester, assigned to this by instruction of the lord Earl of Chester, on the oath of[186] Robert de Staveley, Robert de Neuton, Richard de Woley, [William] Gibonson, Richard de Dewisnape, Robert de Holynworth, Roger del Bothum, William Geffrou, William de Throntelegh,[187] John Lastles, William del Fernylegh and John Hobrode, sworn, who say upon their oath that.[188]

[Mottram, apparently continued]

6.02   Item, they say that John son of John de Radeclyft (Radcliffe) holds in Mottrum one messuage with one garden and one half rood of land by (...........) and renders yearly 1¼d.[189]

6.03   Item, William de Caryngton holds one place called Harop in the same township by knight service and renders yearly 18d. and 1 lb. of cumin.[190]

---

184   For all persons named in this membrane please see P.I. Most statements in the text are supported or illuminated by entries in m. 4 or m. 5 or both, and many are paralleled by similar entries in m. 7. Attention is drawn to these references in the notes below.

185   The feast of the Conversion of St Paul is 25 January, the year was 1360 and the date given is 28 January 1360.

186   For the working list of jurors and their identification see **3.01** and the notes there.

187   In **3.01** this name is given as *Throntel'* in a correction from *Thornclyf*. For the variety of spellings see Earwaker, ii. 146 and P.I.

188   For reasons which may only be conjectured, the scribe next wrote here entries which follow m. 3d: a further two concerning Mottram, and those concerning Hollingworth, etc. This unsatisfactory, and perhaps *ad hoc*, arrangement was rectified in m. 7. See **7.20** with note 285. The # marks were inserted here and in the margin there to guide the scribe as to where to continue copying in the corrected version which was to follow m. 7. See Introduction, pp. xvif., and xxiif.

189   It seems that the scribe intended to insert the service by which this land was held, but failed to do so. See **7.20**, which gives a little more information, but there is no record of any payment of rent in m. 4 or m. 5. In July 1364 John son of John de Radeclif successfully obtained the lands of his wife Margaret, which had been in the Black Prince's hands during her minority. She was heir of Isabel, widow of Sir Thomas Danyers (*B.P.R.,* iii. 470).

190   See **7.21**. This is the Sir William Caryngton referred to in **3.13**. There is no record of any such payment in m. 4 or m. 5, both of which appear to have been written during Sir William's tenure of the lordship of Longdendale. See Introduction and Nevell & Walker, p. 51. Cumin seed was imported from Mediterranean countries and used as a spice.

m. 6

6.04   Item, dicunt quod Johannes de Holynworth' tenet magnam Holynworth per servicium militare et reddit per annum iij s. | [9] iiij d. et faciet *Haghag'* et servicium molendini ut supra, et dat pro Reveyeld vij d. ob. per annum et pro Ward' ij d. ob. et inveniet | [10] unum Judicem et faciet sectam[(w)] ad Curiam de Mottrum de tribus septimanis in iij septimanas.

6.05   Item quod Ricardus de Wolegh tenet | [11] [(x)] terciam partem de [(y)] Parva Holynworth et inveniet unum judicem, et faciet sectam ad Curiam predictam et dat domino per | [12] annum xij d. et dat pro Reveyeld j d. ob. et pro Ward' ob.

6.06   Item quod Cristiana de Holyn' tenet ij partes de eadem | [13] per servicium militare et reddit per annum iij s. et pro eadem et tenet Thorntelegh',[(z)] et pro Reveyeld[(a)] xij d. et pro Ward' iiij d. et faciet *Haghehag'* et opus | [14] molendini et *drive & lede.*

6.07   Item quod Pilippus de Eggerton tenet xl acras terre ibidem et reddit per annum xij d. et pro Reveyeld' | [15] xij d. et pro Ward' iiij d. et faciet ut supra. Item, [[Cristiana predicta tenet]][(b)] |

*A gap of 5–6 cm follows in this membrane, and from here onwards the text (written in a second, smaller hand comparable with **3.02ff.** and **m. 7d**) is cancelled.*

[16] **6.08**   Item per sacramentum Willelmi Geffreu, Johannis Hobrode, Willelmi de Thorntelegh', Roberti de Dewysnape' et aliorum.

6.09   Qui dicunt super sacramentum suum quod Rogerus de | [17] Bothum tenet unum burgagium ibi (!) Tengetwysell', et reddit domino per annum ad festa Sancti Martini et Pentecostes xij d.

(w) *d* struck through.
(x) *p* struck through.
(y) *Magna* struck through.
(z) *et pro eadem et tenet Thorntelegh'* interlineated.
(a) *vj d.* struck through, *xij d.* interlineated.
(b) *Cristiana predicta tenet* struck through.

m. 6

[Hollingworth]
6.04   Item, they say that John de Holynworth holds Great Holynworth by knight service and renders yearly 3s. 4d. and will do haghag and service of the mill as above, and gives for reveyeld 7½d. yearly and for ward 2½d., and he will find one doomsman and will make suit to Mottrum Court every three weeks.[191]
6.05   Item, that Richard de Wolegh holds a third part of Little Holynworth and will find one doomsman, and will make suit to the aforesaid Court and gives to the lord yearly 12d. and gives for reveyeld 1½d. and for ward ½d.[192]
6.06   Item, that Christiana de Holyn holds 2 parts of the same by knight service and renders yearly 3s. and for the same also holds Thorntelegh,[193] and (gives) for reveyeld 12d. and for ward 4d., and she will do haghehag and work of the mill and drive and lead.[194]
6.07   Item that Philip de Eggerton holds 40 acres of land there and renders yearly 12d. and for reveyeld 12d. and for ward 4d., and he will do as above.[195] Item, [[the aforesaid Christiana holds]][196]

From here onwards the text is cancelled.

[Tintwistle]
6.08   Item on the oath of William Geffreu, John Hobrode, William de Thorntelegh, Robert de Dewysnape and others.[197]
6.09   Who say upon their oath that Roger de Bothum holds one burgage there (in) Tengetwysell (Tintwistle), and renders to the lord yearly at the feasts of Saint Martin and Pentecost 12d.[198]

---

191   See **7.23**, which varies the details somewhat, **5.44** and **5.63**. 'Service of the mill as above' appears to refer to **3.08**, and follows after **3.10** and **3.12**, indicating that the scribe was here continuing from m. 3d. For *Haghag*' and other services see **3.08** with note 53 there and Introduction, p. xxv.
192   See **7.24**, which adds 'makes suit to the lord's mill', **4.61–62**, **5.46**, **3.01** and **6.01**.
193   See **7.25**, **4.70**, and **5.45**, as well as **3.01**, and note 35.
194   For *haghehag*' see **3.08** with note 53; for 'work of the mill' see above, note 191. The vernacular expression 'drive & lead' used in the text here appears in **7.25** as 'makes suit to the lord's mill', expressing an obligation to carry grain to and meal from that mill. See **3.06** and Introduction, p. xxiv.
195   See **7.26**. It appears that this land is referred to in **5.59**, where under 'Free tenants in Longdendale' receipt of 12d. is recorded *del Oldefeld in Holynworth*.
196   At this point the scribe wrote 'The aforesaid Christiana holds', presumably about Thorncliffe, but decided instead that the information needed to be included by interlineation in **6.06**, or already had been, and deleted these words.
197   This new heading with a different jury may imply that the information here recorded had been taken on a different occasion. For the first three names on the list see the notes to **3.01**; for Robert de Dewysnape see **6.10** below. It is possible that the jury sworn in here was or represented that of a borough court. What follows in the first place is a catalogue of holders of burgages and other tenements in the failed borough of Tintwistle, noted in a letter from Reginald Bretland of Thorncliffe to Randle Holme of Chester dated 11 April 1665 (MS. Harl. 2039, f. 114). See Nevell & Walker, p. 53.
198   Possibly this was the burgage that Roger's son William paid for in **4.30**. Roger de Bothum also held Great and Little Arnfield and land in Mottram: see **6.45–46**, **4.28–29**, **5.22**; **6.57**, **4.24**; **3.01** with note 33. The list thus begins with the most substantial or important tenant in the borough, who occupied what may have been the principal manor of the lordship.

m. 6

6.10   And that Robert de Dewysnape holds 1 burgage and renders yearly at the same terms 12d.[199]

6.11   And that John le Tieu[200] holds one burgage and renders to the lord yearly at the same terms 10d.

6.12   And that William Nyksone holds one grange and one curtilage and renders to the lord yearly 4d.[201]

6.13   And that the same William holds one toft and renders yearly 2d.

6.14   And that Thomas le Barker holds one burgage and renders yearly at the same terms 12d.[202]

6.15   And that John son of Thomas le Forster[203] holds one little house upon *le Syk*[204] and renders yearly 6d.

6.16   And that Magot Dok's wife holds at will[205] three burgages and renders yearly at the same terms 2s.

6.17   And that Thomas le Barker holds one burgage that was Cobbok's at will and renders to the lord yearly 12d.[206]

6.18   Item, Robert de Dewysnape holds one toft in fee and renders yearly 4d.[207]

6.19   Item, William Geffrou holds one burgage with land adjacent in fee and renders to the lord yearly 2s.[208]

6.20   Item, Robert de Dewysnape holds one parcel of land in fee and renders to the lord yearly 3d.

---

199 See **5.13** and **4.46**. Robert de Dewysnape also held *Aspenforlong* and other properties in Tintwistle. See **6.35**, **4.69**, **5.19**; **6.18**, **6.20** and **4.47**.

200 John le Tieu (also spelled Tuwe), described as 'the Prince's servant', acted as deputy to Sir John Chandos (Steward of the lordship) from 3 April 1359 to Lady Day 1361 when Sir William Caryngton was granted his first lease, and in that capacity rendered account for the lordship throughout that period (SC 6/802/15, m. 1d, and 803/3, m. 4d.) See P.I. There is no record of this rent in m. 4 or m. 5. It may be that he then no longer held this burgage.

201 There is no explicit record of this payment or the next in m. 4 or m. 5. William Nyksone is not listed by that name elsewhere in the manuscripts, but may possibly have been the William le Hune (*or* Hund') in **5.11**. See note 135 there and Appendix, pp. 77, 82.

202 See **4.32** and **5.09**.

203 A John Forster was recorded as operating a boat service between Frodsham and Liverpool between 1366 and 1369 (SC 6/786/7, m. 4, & 786/10, m. 4.) It is not clear whether this was the same person. Neither his name nor the rent is found elsewhere in these mss, but neither are they listed under 'Decay of Rent' in the 1357–61 accounts.

204 Or 'small building' 'above *le Syk*', 'sike' or 'syke' being a northern word for a watercourse. *Le Syk* is referred to also in **6.30**.

205 It is somewhat unusual to find burgages held at will, which presumably means on an annually renewable lease. Burgage tenure is regarded as the most free and secure of all in the middle ages. The explanation here may be that these burgages were vacant after the Black Death of 1348, and let with difficulty. Magot does appear to have been paying a lower than usual rent for them. See **4.41** where the rent is paid by Magot wife of Robert Dokeson, and **5.05** where it is paid by Mag' Dok's daughter. See also Introduction, p. xxxiii and P.I.

206 This may be referred to in **4.44**. The name Cobbok does not appear elsewhere in the mss.

207 For this entry and **6.20** see **4.46**.

208 See **4.48** and perhaps also **5.24**.

m. 6

6.21 Et quod le Herstoncloghouses cum vj acris terre[h] adiacentibus solebat reddere per annum iiij s., sed iacet in decasu.

6.21b Item quod | 25 [[parcella terre est ibidem <Nicholai filii> Willelmi filii Thome Dykeson et reddit domino per annum ij d.]][i]

6.22 Et quod Magota uxor Doke tenet unum croftum et reddit | 26 per annum vj d.[i*]

m. 6d   [The same way up as the recto.]
                              Also cancelled.

[1] **6.23** Item, eadem Magota tenet unum toftum in feodo et reddit domino per annum vj d.

6.24 Item, Robertus filius Doke tenet unum toftum in feodo et reddit per annum vj d.

6.25 Item, Nicholaus | [2] filius Willelmi filij Thome tenet in feodo [j] ij burgagia et iij toftes (!) cum uno crofto[k] pertinenciis et reddit per annum iij s. x d.

6.26 Item, Magota uxor Doke tenet j burgagium et reddit per annum xij d. | [3]

6.26b Item [[eadem Mag' tenet *le Smolterhouses* que fuerunt Johannis filii Willelmi de Hyde et reddit per annum xij d.]][l]

6.27 Item, Henricus le Wylde tenet j burgagium in feodo | [4] eo quod ad terminum vite uxoris sue, cum uno tofto, et reddit per annum xxj d.

6.28 Item, Henricus le Smyth de Stokport tenet unum messuagium cum quadam | [5] fabrica in feodo et reddit per annum vj d.

6.29 Item, Henricus le Wyld tenet unum burgagium cum *le Rodefeld* ad voluntatem et reddit domino per annum viij s. vj d. | [6]

6.30 Item, unum mesuagium est super *le Syk* quod fuit Roberti le Smyth et reddit per annum vij d.

(h) *terra* first written struck through, *vj acris terre* interlineated.

(i) *parcella terre est ibidem <Nicholai filii> Willelmi filii Thome Dykeson et reddit domino per annum ij d.* first written struck through, with the explanatory note *quia alibi* interlineated above *terre.*

(i*) *per annum vj d.* added below end of line.

(j) *in feodo* interlineated.

(k) *uno crofto* interlineated.

(l) *eadem Mag' tenet le Smolterhouses que fuerunt Johannis filii Willelmi de Hyde et reddit per annum xij d.* first written struck through, with the explanatory note *quia inferius* interlineated above *tenet.*

m. 6

6.21   And that *le Herstoncloghouses*[209] with 6 acres of land adjacent used to render 4s. yearly, but is lying in decay.
6.21b Item that [[there is a parcel of land there of Nicholas son of William son of Thomas Dykeson and it renders to the lord yearly 2d.]][210]
6.22   And that Magot Dok's wife holds one croft and renders yearly 6d.[211]

m. 6d
Also cancelled.
6.23   Item, the same Magot holds one toft in fee and renders to the lord yearly 6d.
6.24   Item, Robert Dok's son holds one toft in fee and renders yearly 6d.[212]
6.25   Item, Nicholas son of William son of Thomas holds in fee 2 burgages and 3 tofts with appurtenances (one croft) and renders yearly 3s. 10d.[213]
6.26   Item, Magot Dok's wife holds one burgage and renders yearly 12d.[214]
6.26b Item [[the same Mag holds *le Smolterhouses* which were John son of William de Hyde's and renders yearly 12d.]][215]
6.27   Item, Henry le Wylde holds 1 burgage in fee so far as to the end of his wife's life, with one toft, and renders yearly 21d.[216]
6.28   Item, Henry le Smyth of Stokport holds one messuage with a certain forge in fee and renders yearly 6d.[217]
6.29   Item, Henry le Wyld holds one burgage with *le Rodefeld* at will and renders to the lord yearly 8s. 6d.[218]
6.30   Item, one messuage is upon *le Syk* which was Robert le Smyth's and renders yearly 7d.[219]

209 See **5.25** with note 149 and Introduction, p. xx.
210 Here the scribe first wrote *There is a parcel of land there of Nicholas son of Thomas Dykeson and it renders to the lord yearly 2d.*, but later crossed it through with the note *because elsewhere*, referring presumably to **6.25** below.
211 For this and the next entry see **4.41**. For Dok's family see Introduction, p. xxxiii and P.I.
212 See **4.42**, which records a Martinmas term rent of 3d. for a burgage.
213 See **5.06** and **6.21b** above.
214 See **4.41**, where the rent is paid by Magot wife of Robert Dokeson, and **5.07**, where it is paid by Mag Dok's daughter.
215 This entry was deleted with the note *because below*, perhaps referring to **6.32**. See **4.41** with note 100. Despite the deletion, the very name *le Smolterhouses*, presumably either a local or an early form of 'Smelterhouses', indicates the existence of structures used specifically for the smelting industry in Tintwistle at this date. Although the metal may have been lead, perhaps iron is more likely. Note the number of smiths mentioned below and in other membranes.
216 See **4.35** and **5.08**.
217 This may be the property referred to in **4.40**, where a Martinmas term receipt is recorded from Thomas Faber, i.e. the smith.
218 See **4.36** and **5.03**.
219 See **5.16**, where he is called 'Robert le Smyth the elder'.

m. 6d

6.31   Item, una placea cum curtilagio que fuit Symonis le Smith | [7] iacet in deca-
su et solebat reddere per annum ix d.
6.32   Item, [(m)] Johannes filius Willelmi de Hyde tenet vj burgagia et ix acras terre
in feodo[(n)] et reddit per annum ad | [8] eosdem terminos xiiij s. v d.
6.33   Item, idem Johannes tenet unam placeam iuxta molendinum et solet (*or*
solebat)[(o)] reddere per annum vj d.
6.34   Item, Johannes Hobrode tenet j burgagium cum quodam tofto in feodo et |
[9] reddit per annum xvj d.
6.35   Item Robertus de Dewysnape tenet j burgagium cum terr(is) adiacent(ibus)
ad voluntatem et reddit per annum viij s.
6.36   Item, quoddam burgagium quod fuit | [10] Roberti le Merser iacet in decasu
et solebat reddere per annum xij d.
6.37   Item, j burgagium quod fuit Willelmi le Stiwardesson iacet in decasu et
solebat reddere per annum xij d. |
[11] **6.38**   Item, Ricardus de Halghton tenet *le Wallefeld* ad voluntatem et reddit
per annum ix s.
6.39   Item, Johannes Hobberode tenet *le Wallecroft* ad voluntatem et reddit | [12]
per annum iij s.
6.40   Item, idem Johannes et Thomas le Barker tenent unam placeam terre ibidem ad voluntatem et reddunt per annum x s.
6.41   Item, Willelmus de Thorn | [13] ley tenet j burgagium cum adiacentibus ter-
ris[(p)] ibidem ad voluntatem et reddit per annum xiiij s. vj d.
6.42   Item, est ibi *le Heewodeheyghe* que solet reddere per annum xij s. |
[14] **6.43**   Item, Johannes le Tieu tenet unum pratum ad voluntatem et reddit per
annum xiijj d.

(m) *quod parva fabrica* first written struck through.
(n) *in feodo* interlineated.
(o) *sol'* interlineated.
(p) *j burgagium cum adiacentibus terris* interlineated.

m. 6d

6.31   Item, one plot with a curtilage which was Symon le Smith's is lying in decay and used to render yearly 9d.[220]

6.32   Item, John son of William de Hyde holds 6 burgages and 9 acres of land in fee and renders yearly at the same terms 14s. 5d.[221]

6.33   Item, the same John holds a plot next to the mill and used to render yearly 6d.[222]

6.34   Item, John Hobrode holds 1 burgage with a certain toft in fee and renders yearly 16d.[223]

6.35   Item, Robert de Dewysnape holds 1 burgage with lands adjacent at will and renders yearly 8s.[224]

6.36   Item, a certain burgage which was Robert le Merser's is lying in decay and used to render yearly 12d.[225]

6.37   Item, 1 burgage which was William le Stiwardesson's is lying in decay and used to render yearly 12d.[226]

6.38   Item, Richard de Halghton holds *le Wallefeld* at will and renders yearly 9s.[227]

6.39   Item, John Hobberode holds *le Wallecroft* at will and renders yearly 3s.[228]

6.40   Item, the same John and Thomas le Barker hold one plot of land there at will and render yearly 10s.[229]

6.41   Item, William de Thornley[230] holds 1 burgage with lands adjacent there at will and renders yearly 14s. 6d.

6.42   Item, there is there *le Heewodeheyghe* which is accustomed to render yearly 12s.[231]

6.43   Item, John le Tieu[232] holds one meadow at will and renders yearly 14d.

220   See **5.17** with note 141. This property first appears under 'Decay of Rent' in the 1359–60 account (SC 6/802/17, m. 5) and is repeated in that of 1360–March 1361 (SC 6/803/3, m. 5.)
221   See **4.43** with note 102, and **5.12** with note 136. See also above, note 58, p. 19 and P.I.
222   There is no separate record of this payment in m. 4 or m. 5.
223   See **4.34**, **5.10** and **3.01**.
224   See **4.69** and **5.19** from which it appears that the lands mentioned were called *aspenforlong*. See **6.08** and **6.10** above, and also note 143, p. 35.
225   There is no record of this name and payment in m. 4 or m. 5. The land late Robert Mercer's appears under 'Decay of Rent' in the accounts throughout the period 1358–61.
226   The burgage late William Stywardessone's is identified under 'Decay of Rent' in the 1357–59 accounts, but not that of 1359–60, implying that between 28 January and Michaelmas 1360 it had been re-occupied. It may perhaps be the one held by Robert le Smyth in **5.15**.
227   See **4.38–39** and **5.04** with notes *ad loc.*, and P.I.
228   This land may be included in his Martinmas term payment of 3s. 7d.: see **4.33**. *Wall Croft* was still a Tintwistle field-name c. 1845 (Dodgson, i. 328).
229   See **4.31** and **4.33**. For Thomas le Barker see also **6.14** with **4.32** and **5.09**, and **6.17**.
230   See **4.45** and **5.18**. This is another variant of the spelling of his name: see **3.01** with note 35, **6.01** with note 187, and P.I.
231   Presumably identical with *Ewodeheye*. See **5.21**, where 12s. rent is listed but no tenant named, and note 145. In **4.37** a Robert Godard pays an otherwise unexplained Martinmas term rent of 6s., which may relate to this land.
232   See **6.11** above, with note 200. There is no record of this rent in m. 4 or m. 5.

m. 6d

6.44   Item, Willelmus le Mulner tenet ij mesuagia cum terra adiacenti ad voluntatem | [15] et reddit per annum xj s.

6.45   Item, Rogerus del Bothum tenet Parvam[(q)] Arnefeld ad voluntatem et reddit per annum xx s., reddit pro Revegald et Ward' iiij d.[(r)]

6.46   Item, idem Rogerus tenet magnam Arnefeld | [16] ad voluntatem et reddit per annum xxvj s., pro Revegaldo et Ward' viij d.[(s)]

6.47   Item, Johannes Lastles, Simon le Muleward, Willelmus del Fernylegh' et Adam de Gaunt'[(ss)] et | [17] Thomas le Prestessone tenent Mukelhurst et Lytelhurst' ad voluntatem et reddunt per annum vj marcas et dimidiam.

6.48   Item, Adam de Harop' tenet j mesuagium | [18] et terram adjacentem ad voluntatem in Mottrum et reddit per annum iiij s. iij d.

6.49   Item, Stephanus de Harop' Junior[(t)] tenet j mesuagium cum terra adiacenti ad voluntatem | [19] et reddit per annum iiij s. iij d. et reddunt pro Ward' et Reveyeld' j d. qu.[(u)]

6.50   Item, Henricus Gybon' tenet j mesuagium cum terra adiacenti ad voluntatem et reddit per annum iij s. et reddit pro Ward' et Reveyeld iiij d.[(v)]

6.51   Item, Jordanus del Haghe | [20] tenet j mesuagium cum terra adiacenti ad voluntatem et reddit per annum iiij s. ix d. et reddit pro Ward' et Reveyeld iiij d.[(w)]

6.52   Item, Stephanus de Harop' senior tenet j mesuagium cum terra adiacenti | [21] ad voluntatem et reddit per annum iiij s.

(q)   *Parvam* interlineated.
(r)   *reddit pro Revegald et Ward' iiij d.* interlineated without 'caret'.
(s)   *pro Revegaldo et Ward' viiij d.* interlineated.
(ss) Or perhaps *Gamit'*.
(t)   *Junior* interlineated.
(u)   *et reddunt pro Ward' et Reveyeld' j d. qu.* interlineated.
(v)   *et reddit pro Ward' et Reveyeld iiij d.* interlineated.
(w)   *et reddit pro Ward' et Reveyeld iiij d.* interlineated.

m. 6d

6.44   Item, William le Mulner holds 2 messuages with land adjacent at will and renders yearly 11s.[233]

[Arnfield]

6.45   Item, Roger del Bothum holds Little Arnefeld at will and renders yearly 20s., he renders for revegald and ward 4d.

6.46   Item, the same Roger holds Great Arnefeld at will and renders yearly 26s., for revegald and ward 8d.[234]

[Micklehurst and Littlehurst]

6.47   Item, John Lastles,[235] Simon le Muleward,[236] William del Fernylegh,[237] and Adam de Gaunt[238] and Thomas le Prestessone[239] hold Mukelhurst[240] and Lytelhurst[241] at will and render yearly 6 marks and a half.[242]

[Mottram]

6.48   Item, Adam de Harop holds 1 messuage with land adjacent at will in Mottrum and renders yearly 4s. 3d.[243]

6.49   Item, Stephen de Harop the younger holds 1 messuage with land adjacent at will and renders yearly 4s. 3d. and they render for ward and reveyeld 1¼d.[244]

6.50   Item, Henry Gybon holds 1 messuage with land adjacent at will and renders yearly 3s., and renders for ward and reveyeld 4d.[245]

6.51   Item, Jordan del Haghe holds 1 messuage with land adjacent at will and renders yearly 4s. 9d., and renders for ward and reveyeld 4d.[246]

6.52   Item, Stephen de Harop the elder holds 1 messuage with land adjacent[247] at will and renders yearly 4s.

233   See **4.27** with note 87 and **5.23**.
234   See **4.28–29**, **5.22** and **3.01** with note 33. In **3.05** Arnfield is called a manor which is let at farm, and it was here that the boon services were to be (or had been) performed.
235   The juror of **3.01**, **6.01** (and **7.01**), though his name does not appear in m. 4. See note 36.
236   See **4.54**, where his occupation is given in Latin. This name may imply the existence by this time of a mill somewhere in the Tame valley, perhaps in the Micklehurst area.
237   Another juror of **3.01**, **6.01**, and **7.01**: see note 37. It is likely that he is referred to in **4.51** by the patronymic *Symeson*.
238   See **4.50**.
239   Further identified in **4.52** as Thomas son of Richard the Chaplain.
240   Since 1974 Micklehurst, together with Buckton Castle (referred to above, **3.02** and note 39) has been within the Metropolitan Borough of Tameside, Greater Manchester. See Nevell & Walker, pp. 10, 48.
241   Littlehurst is a vanished place-name, presumably near Micklehurst since the names imply comparison. See Dodgson, i. 322. In the 1357–62 accounts (SC 6/802/15, m. 1; 6/802/17, m. 5; 6/803/5, m. 2) Arnfield, Micklehurst and Littlehurst are all referred to as hamlets of Tintwistle.
242   The rent from this joint tenure appears as one item in **5.38**, but in **4.50–54** the separate Martinmas term rents amount to £2 4s. 2½d., which would produce an annual rent of £4 8s. 5d.
243   See **4.16**, **4.18** and **5.35**.
244   These amounts tally with those recorded in **4.17–18**, but not with those in **5.35**, which may indicate that they then occupied less land. From **4.18** it is clear that the ward and reveyeld are from both the brothers.
245   See **4.06–07** and **5.30**. In **4.08–09** it is clear that this Henry was then also at charges for part of Sir John Hyde's land.
246   See **4.12–13** and **5.32**.
247   See **4.02** and **5.29** where this holding is named *le holehous'*: see note 151, p. 37.

m. 6d

6.53   Item, Watkyn Rowessone tenet j mesuagium cum terra adiacenti ad voluntatem et reddit per annum vj s. iij d. et reddit pro Ward' et Reveyeld iiij d.[(x)]

6.54   Item, Willelmus | [22] del Wharell tenet j mesuagium cum terra adiacenti ad
voluntatem et reddit per annum ij s. x d. et reddit pro Ward' et Reveyeld ij d.
ob.[(y)]

6.55   Item, Willelmus filius Johannis tenet j mesuagium cum terra adiacenti ad |
[23] voluntatem et reddit per annum ix s. vj d. unde Reveyeld et Ward' iiij d.[(z)]

6.56   Item, Radulfus Tyllessone tenet (Thomerode)[(a)] ad voluntatem et reddit per
annum ij s.

6.57   Item, Rogerus del Bothum | [24] tenet j mesuagium cum terr(a) adiacent(i) ad
voluntatem et reddit per annum iiij s.

6.58   Item, Hugo del Ruggeway tenet j mesuagium cum terr(a) adiacent(i) ad vol-
untatem et | [25] reddit per annum xiiij s.

6.59   Item, idem Hugo pro Ward' et Reveyeld iij d. qu.

6.60   Item, Thomas le Foucher [(b)] tenet Parvam Rudyng' ad voluntatem et reddit
per annum | [26] ij s. Item
            Remainder of line blank, then a small gap.

[27] **6.61**   Memorandum quod tenentes ad voluntatem de Parva Arnefeld et Magna[(c)]
Arnefeld invenient iiij homines ad opus molendini quociens necesse fuerit.
            Gap of about 1 cm.
[28] **6.62**   Item dicunt quod Ricardus filius Roberti de Eton' qui est etatis xv anno-
rum tenet villam de Wernyth de domino de Longeden' per servicium | [29] militare. |

(x)   *et reddit pro Ward' et Reveyeld iiij d.* interlineated.
(y)   *et reddit pro Ward' et Reveyeld ij d. ob.* interlineated.
(z)   *unde Reveyeld et Ward' iiij d.* interlineated.
(a)   This (otherwise unknown) place-name may be incompletely transcribed since there is a mark of
       contraction through the ascender of the *h*.
(b)   Or *Foncher*.
(c)   *tenentes de Parva Arnefeld et Magna* interlineated, then *ad voluntatem* interlineated above that.

m. 6d

6.53 Item, Watkyn Rowessone[248] holds 1 messuage with land adjacent at will and renders yearly 6s. 3d. and renders for ward and reveyeld 4d.
6.54 Item, William del Wharell holds 1 messuage with land adjacent at will and renders yearly 2s. 10d., and renders for ward and reveyeld 2½d.[249]
6.55 Item, William son of John holds 1 messuage with land adjacent at will and renders yearly 9s. 6d., of which reveyeld and ward 4d.[250]
6.56 Item, Ralph Tyllessone[251] holds (Thomerode)[252] at will and renders yearly 2s.
6.57 Item, Roger del Bothum holds 1 messuage with land adjacent at will and renders yearly 4s.[253]
6.58 Item, Hugh del Ruggeway holds 1 messuage with land adjacent at will and renders yearly 14s.[254]
6.59 Item, the same Hugh for ward and revegeld 3¼d.
6.60 Item, Thomas le Foucher[255] holds Little Rudyng[256] at will and renders yearly 2s. Item,

[Arnfield]
6.61 It is to be remembered that the tenants at will of Little Arnefeld and Great Arnefeld will find 4 men for work of the mill as often as it shall be necessary.[257]

[Werneth]
6.62 Item they say that Richard son of Robert de Eton, who is 15 years of age, holds the township of Wernyth from the lord of Longeden' by knight service.[258]

248 This is almost certainly Wadkyn del Haghe (**4.19–20**) and Walter son of Ralph (**5.33**). Rowe appears to be a variant spelling of Roe (as in Roe Cross), another form of Ralph. Cf. Old Roe's tomb in Mottram Church (Earwaker, ii. 119). See P.I.
249 See **4.22–23** and **5.31**, which, however, records a rent of 7s., presumably for more land.
250 This appears to be William de Godelegh: see **4.14–15** for closely tallying Martinmas term payments. This land may also be referred to in **5.20**, though the rent there is 11s. 4d., perhaps for more land. It appears from CCCIR 1373 that Sir William Caryngton, then farmer of the lordship of Longdendale, between the years 1361 and 1373 demolished *inter alia* a messuage in Mottram worth 20s. that was William de Godlye's. See P.I.
251 See **4.58–59**. The latter seems to be the Martinmas term rent for this property.
252 This (possibly incompletely deciphered) place-name does not appear elsewhere in these manuscripts, though the relevant tenant and rent appear in **4.59**. The place has not been identified. The mark of contraction through the ascender of the *h* would normally indicate the omission of a letter or letters somewhere in the name.
253 See **4.24**; **3.01** with note 33, **6.01**, (**7.01**); **6.45–46**, **4.28–29** and **5.22**; **6.09**; **6.61**. This property at Mottram may have been at Botham's Hall.
254 For this entry and the next see the payments made by Richard de Riggeway, **4.04–05** and **5.34**. The discrepancy of the names presumably indicates that those later payments were made by another member of Hugh's family.
255 See **4.21**. The name can also be read as *Foncher*, though *Foucher* is found in Derbyshire (Sue Brown, Ranulf Higden Society, private communication).
256 The field-name 'Riddings' is found in Mottram township (Dodgson, i. 316).
257 This work is first referred to in **3.08**. See **6.04** and **6.06** above with notes 191 and 194.
258 See **7.22**. Werneth is outside the bounds of Mottram Parish, to the south-west of Mottram and Hattersley. See Map, p. viii, Nevell & Walker, p. 48, and P.I.

m. 6d

Gap of over 1 cm.

[30] **6.63   Longeden'** + Solebat reddere xij li. est in manu domini, et dimittitur ad firmam a festo Sancti Martini anno xxxiij usque idem festum proxime sequens | [31] pro xij li.

6.64   Et habebunt bek' de shrag'[(d)] de Holyn racionabiliter cum pannagio herbagio et tolnetis, et cum escapuris per totam Longeden' |

[32] **6.65**   Memorandum de piscaria de Edrowe dimissa ad firmam Petro de Arden[(e)] a festo Sancti Michelis anno xxxiij usque idem festum proxime sequens pro vj s. viij d. del *Rontandebrok* | [33] usque *Salterbrok'*.[(f)]

(d)   The reviser is indebted to Mr Peter Gaskins of the Ranulf Higden Society for kindly re-examining this difficult entry by ultra-violet light and recognising in *bek'* the *k* where previously only the upright *l* had been seen. For discussion see footnote to translation opposite.

(e)   *Petro de Arden* interlineated.

(f)   *del Rontandebrok* (or *Routandebrok*, *Rontaudebrok*, or *Routaudebrok*) added after *vj s. viij d.*, and *usque Salterbrok'* below on the next line.

m. 6d

6.63 **Longeden'** used to render £12, is in the lord's hand, and is leased at fixed rent from Martinmas in the 33rd year (1359) until the same feast next following for £12.[259]

6.64 And they shall have the *becage* of the bushes (or scrub-land) of Holyn reasonably with pannage, pasture and tolls, and with fines for straying animals through the whole of Longeden'[260]

6.65 It is to be remembered concerning the fishery of Edrow (Etherow) let at fixed rent to Peter de Arden from Michaelmas in the 33rd year (1359) until the same feast next following for 6s. 8d.[261] from Rontandebrok[262] to Salterbrok.[263]

---

259 This item refers to the farm of the agistment of Longdendale, worth £12 in the 1357–61 accounts (SC 6/802/15, m. 1; 802/17, m. 5; 803/3, m. 5). See **2.10** with notes 3 and 12; **3.01** with note 34; **5.39–40**, and Tables 1 and 2 pp. xxxviii–xxxix.

260 This entry may be a continuation of **6.63**. Clearly *bek' de shrag'* defines the first of the additional benefits or advantages which the tenants of the farm mentioned above shall have. In this context *bek'* is most reasonably interpreted as an alternative suspended form of the locally-recorded word *becagium* defined by *D.M.L.* as 'payment for pasturage of cattle in forest (Macclesfield)' with citations from Ministers' Accounts of 1330 (SC 6/802/1, r. 2); 1352 (2) (802/6 and 802/7, m. 1); and 1362 (803/5, r. 1) using in two cases the spelling *begagio*. In the 1362 example it is also associated with pannage. It is unclear whether *shrag'* (the *a* in this case being tall and distinctly written) may be a variant of the English place-name element *shrog* (listed for both Cheshire and Yorkshire West Riding), 'scrub-land', or the word *shrag* or *shragge* which *O.E.D.* (2nd edn) defines as occasionally meaning 'a bush or low tree', providing the 1605 citation 'A kynd of breach or valey down a slope from the syde of a hill, where comonly shragges and trees do grow' — a description equally appropriate to the Hollingworth landscape.

261 See **2.12** with note 14. For Peter de Arderne see P.I.

262 This brook, not yet identified, was presumably the western boundary of the lordship of Longdendale, and would have been a tributary of the Etherow on its northern side.

263 Salter's Brook was the Cheshire boundary with the West Riding of Yorkshire at the upper end of Longdendale. See Plates 13 and 14, p. lii.

m. 7

[Parchment (flesh side), c. 47 cm. high × c. 24.5 cm. wide.]

ANOTHER CANCELLED DRAFT OF THE (1360) EXTENT
Left margin ruled at c. 2.5 cm. More formally written than m. 6, but similarly
cancelled by a line struck more or less vertically. Headings in left margin are set
out below above their respective paragraphs. Line endings are shown by / and
lines numbered.

¹ **7.01**   [...Sancti Pauli Apostoli |
² [... ....] Justiciar(ij) Cestrie |
³ [...]rie ad hoc |
⁴ [..........] per sacramentum Roberti de Staveley [...
....] Gibonsone | ⁵ [.........................]wisnape, Roberti de
Holynworth' Rogeri del [...............] Geffrou', Willelmi [.....]elegh' [......] | ⁶ Lastles,
Willelmi del Fernylegh' et Johannis Hobberode, juratorum [qui] dicunt super
sacramentum suum quod |

⁷ **7.02**   In primis⁽ᵍ⁾ Est ibidem unum castrum dirutum vocatum Buckeden castel-
lum et nullius valoris. [[et est ibidem una aula | ⁸ una camera et una capella que
dimittuntur ad firmam reddunt per annum]]⁽ʰ⁾ |

Neuton'
⁹ **7.03** Item Robertus de Neuton tenet Manerium de Neuton per servicium militare
et per servicia inveniendi | ¹⁰ pro quolibet tenente suo terminario unum hominem
per tres dies in autumpno ad unum repastum per diem, videlicet panem | ¹¹ butirum
et lac apud Manerium de Arnefeld' quod [...] tempore
quadragesimali pro quolibet t(enente) | ¹² [....... unam c]arucam per tres dies ad
unum pastum [............] una caruca per diem vj cakes [..........] | ¹³ [..........
...................................] Et dominus in[veniet ....] ad custus
dictorum ten(entium) et unam domum [... ....
...........................] etc. | ¹⁴ imponend' tempore [......] ipso et tenentibus suis fac(ere)
sectam ad mol(endinum) domini⁽ⁱ⁾ |

(g) *In primis* interlineated.
(h) *et est ibidem una aula | ⁸ una camera et una capella que dimittuntur ad firmam reddunt per*
   annum struck through, with the superscript note *quod inferius.*
(i) This line, from *imponend'* to *domini*, is in a different hand.

m. 7

ANOTHER CANCELLED DRAFT OF THE (1360) EXTENT[264]

7.01 [...] of Saint Paul the Apostle [... ....] of the Justiciar of Chester [...] to this [...............] on the oath of Robert de Staveley, [...] [...] Gibonsone [........................... De]wisnape, Robert de Holynworth, Roger del [........................] Geffrou, William [.....]elegh [......] Lastles, William del Fernylegh and John Hobberode, sworn, [who] say upon their oath that[265]

7.02 Firstly, there is there one ruined fort called Buckeden (Buckton) Castle, and of no value.[266] [[And there is there one hall one chamber and one chapel which are let at fixed rent, render yearly]][267]

Neuton[268] (Newton)
7.03 Item Robert de Neuton holds the manor of Neuton by knight service and by the services of finding for each termor tenant of his one man for three days in harvest time at one meal a day, that is to say bread, butter and milk at the manor of Arnefeld which [............. ....] in Lenten time for each t(enant) [.. .... one] plough for three days at one meal [..... ... .] one plough per day 6 cakes [.. ....] And the lord will find [.... ... ...] at the costs of the said ten(ants) and one house [... ....] etc.[269] imposing at the time [..............] on him and his tenants to make suit to the lord's mill.[270]

---

264 The text of what can be recovered of this membrane should be compared with membranes 3 and 6. Attention is drawn to the parallel entries in the notes below.
265 See **3.01** and **6.01**.
266 See **3.02**.
267 See **3.03**. The deletion of this entry is explained by the superscript note *because below*. This may perhaps refer to part of **7.03** now lost (see above, n. 40) or perhaps more probably to the substance of **6.45–46** which in the final version would follow in its appropriate place. The elliptical expression is one of the indications that this was not intended as the final complete version of the extent.
268 See **3.05**.
269 This *etc*. (like others to be found later) is another indication that this was not intended as the final version of the extent, but as a draft.
270 In the other membranes there is no entry comparable to this unfortunately defective last additional note to help with its interpretation.

m. 7

Ma[tte]legh'

[15] **7.04**   [....] dicunt quod W. [.. ..]de ten(uit)[(j)] medietatem Manerij de Mattelegh' et qui obijt inde seisitus | [16] et descendit ius eiusdem [medi]etatis Ricardo filio ipsius Willelmi.   Et idem Ricardus obijt inde seisitus [et ius] | [17] eiusdem medietatis desc[endit] [...........] fratri eiusdem Ricardi, et Johannes de Hyde Chivaler tenet eamdem medietatem, | [18] quo iure ignorant. Et [ten]etur eadem medietas de domino de Longedendale per servicium militare.

7.05   Item dicunt | [19] quod Johannes de Hyde, Ch[ivaler, ...] eiusdem Manerii per servicium militare.

7.06   Item dicunt quod Henricus filius R[oberti] | [20] de Holynworth' [.................... ....] idem servicium [et] per servicium iiij s. per annum de toto Mane[rio] | [21] predicto et per [.......................................] War[.....................]ehag' videlicet inveniend' vj homines per unum diem | [22] [....] pastu [.....................]ad faciend' ha[....... ....] quolibet anno et per servicium faciendi opus terrenum | [23] [ad molend'] de Tynget[wyssell ....] et fac[.....] sectam ad dictam molend(inam) [.......................] | [24] sectam ad Curiam de Mottrum et inveniendi [..] Judicatores in eadem, etcetera.[(k)]

[God]legh

[26] **7.07**   Item dicunt quod Johannes de Hyde, Chivaler, tenet medietatem Manerij de Godlegh per servicium militare et reddit domino j d. per annum.[(l)]

7.08   Item Howel ap | [27] Oweyn Voyl et her(es) Willelmi de Tranemell' tenent quartam partem eiusdem ville per servicium militare.[(m)]

7.09   Item fil(ia) et heres Galfridi de | [28] Honford' tenet aliam quartam partem dicte ville et est infra etatem, videlicet etatis[(n)] iiij[or] annorum per servicium militare.

7.10   Item, | [29] Robertus le Warde de Godelegh' tenet unum Mesuagium et dimidiam[(o)] carucatam terre in eadem villa, an tenet de | [30] domino de Longedendale an de aliis ignoratur, set facit *Haghag'* et opus Molendini ut supra. |

[31] **7.11**   Item, Johannes filius Johannis de Godlegh' tenet unum Mesuagium et viginti et quatuor acras terre in eadem villa et reddit per | [32] annum j d.[(p)] |

(j)   Although the з-like sign written after *ten* very frequently indicates *tenet*, this scribe has here used it indiscriminately in place of the tittle found in the previous draft **3.06** and recorded in Sir Henry Spelman's *Archaismus Graphicus* (1606) as signifying both *tenet* and *tenuit* (the sense required here). Cf. *inter alia* MS. Harl. 6353, 7.

(k)   *Et facient sectam ad molend* | [25] *inum de Tyng'* next written struck through.

(l)   *per servicium militare* first written struck through, *per servicium militare et reddit domino j d. per annum* interlineated in a different hand.

(m)   *per servicium militare* interlineated in the second hand (hand 2) mentioned in the note above. Cf. also note (y) below.

(n)   *etatis* interlineated.

(o)   *unam* first written struck through, *dimid'* interlineated.

(p)   *Item, Johannes de Hyde, Chivaler, reddit per annum pro tenentibus antedictis in eadem villa j d.* next written struck through.

m. 7

Ma[tte]legh (Matley)

7.04   [....] they say that W. [de Hy]de held half of the manor of Mattelegh and who died seised of it, and the right to the same [half] descended to Richard son of that William. And the same Richard died seised of it [and the right] to the same half descended to [....] brother of the same Richard, and John de Hyde, knight, holds the same half, by what right they do not know. And the same half is held from the lord of Longedendale by knight service. [271]

7.05   Item they say that John de Hyde, knight, [...] of the same manor by knight service.[272]

7.06   Item they say that Henry son of R[obert] de Holynworth [..... ....
....] the same service [and] by the service of 4s. a year from the whole manor aforesaid and by [...... ....] War[...... ....] ehag that is to say of finding 6 men for one day [........ .] meal [..... ....
....] making ha[....... ... ...] each year and by the service of mak-ing earthwork [at the mill of] Tynget[wysell ....
.......] and [of] making suit to the said mill [... .. ..] suit to the Court of Mottrum and of finding [..] Doomsmen in the same, etc.[273]

[God]legh (Godley)

7.07   Item they say that John de Hyde, knight, holds half of the manor of Godlegh by knight service and renders to the lord 1d. yearly.

7.08   Item Howel ap Oweyn Voyl and the heir of William de Tranemell hold a quarter of the same township by knight service.

7.09   Item the daughter and heiress of Geoffrey de Honford holds another quar-ter of the said township and is under age, that is to say 4 years of age, by knight service. [274]

7.10   Item Robert le Warde de Godelegh holds one messuage and half a caru-cate of land in the same township, whether he holds it from the lord of Longedendale or from others is not known, but he does Haghag and work of the mill as above.[275]

7.11   Item John son of John de Godlegh holds one messuage and twenty-four acres of land in the same township and renders yearly 1d.[276]

---

271 See **3.06**.
272 See **3.07**.
273 See **3.08** and **4.68**.
274 For **7.07–7.09** see **3.09**.
275 See **3.10**.
276 See **3.11**. Here next the scribe first wrote *Item, John de Hyde, knight, renders yearly for the aforesaid tenants in the same township 1d.*, but later struck it through, presumably recognising that a more correct interpretation of **3.11b** was already included in **7.07**.

m. 7

Hattreslegh'

³³ **7.12**   Item dicunt quod Ricardus de Eton' qui est etatis quindecim annorum tenet medietatem Manerij de | ³⁴ Hattreslegh' per descensum hereditarium et per servicium militare et per servicia metendi in autumpno per tres dies | ³⁵ et in quadragesima cum caruca per tres dies ad unum pastum ut supra. Et fac(it) *Haghag* per tres dies | ³⁶ ut supra et opera molendini ut supra.

7.13   Item, Willelmus de Carington' Chivaler tenet aliam medietatem | ³⁷ dicte ville per eadem servicia ut supra et predicti fac(iunt) sectam ad molendin(um) domini et sectam ad Curiam de Mottrum.^(q) Et invenient unum Judicatorem in eadem Curia.^(r) |

³⁸ **7.14**   Et ijdem Ricardus et Willelmus reddunt domino per annum pro Reveyeld' et Warde ix d. |

Mottrum

³⁹ **7.15**   Item dicunt quod Johannes de Hyde Chivaler, Howel ap Oweyn Voyl et her(es) Willelmi de Tranemoll' | ⁴⁰ et fil(ia) Galfridi de Honford' tenent in Mottrum in *le Haghe* unum mesuagium et unam carucatam terre | ⁴¹ per servicium militare et reddunt per annum iiij s.

7.16   Item Johannes de Hyde Chivaler tenet in eadem unum Mesuagium | ⁴² et septem acras terre per servicium militare et reddit domino xiij d. per annum.

7.17   Idem Johannes de Hyde tenet | ⁴³ in eadem unam placeam terre vocatam *le Grenehouse*^(s) et reddit domino pro Reveyeld' per annum iij d. et pro | ⁴⁴ Warde j d., et facit sectam ad molendinum domini pro eodem tenemento.^(t)

7.18   Item Ricardus de Dewisnape tenet unum | ⁴⁵ Mesuagium et medietatem unius bovate terre ibidem^(u) et reddit per annum v s. ij d. et facit sectam ad molendinum domini.^(v)

7.19   Item, Radulfus de Wolegh tenet | ⁴⁶ ibidem unum Mesuagium et octo acras terre per servicia predicta preter sectam molendini ^(w) et reddit per annum iij s.

7.20   Item dicunt quod Johannes filius Johannis de | ⁴⁷ ^(x)Radeclyf' tenet ibidem unum mesuagium cum j gardino et dimidiam rodam terre et reddit per annum j d. qu. Et facit sectam ad molendinum domini.^(y)

(q) *et predicti fac(iunt) sectam ad molendin(um) domini et sectam ad Curiam de Mottrum* interlineated, possibly in a different hand.

(r) *de Mottrum* first written after *Curia* struck through, then *eadem* interlineated below the line before *Curia*.

(s) Or *Grevehouse*.

(t) *pro eodem tenemento* interlineated.

(u) *ibidem* interlineated.

(v) *et facit sectam ad molendinum domini* interlineated in hand 2.

(w) *preter sectam molendini* interlineated in hand 2.

(x) In left margin opposite *Radeclyf* a large sign # .

(y) *Et facit sectam ad molendinum domini* interlineated. Entries **7.20–21** appear to have been inserted later, being written in a smaller hand. They may be in hand 2 which wrote **m. 7d**.

m. 7

Hattreslegh (Hattersley)

7.12   Item they say that Richard de Eton who is fifteen years of age holds half of the manor of Hattreslegh by hereditary descent and by knight service and by the services of reaping in harvest time for three days and (ploughing) in Lent with a plough for three days at one meal as above. And he does Haghag for three days as above and works of the mill as above.[277]

7.13   Item William de Carington, knight, holds the other half of the said township by the same services as above and the aforesaid[278] make suit to the lord's mill and suit to the court of Mottrum. And they will find one doomsman in the same Court.

7.14   And the same Richard and William render to the lord yearly for reveyeld and warde 9d.[279]

Mottrum (Mottram)

7.15   Item they say that John de Hyde, knight, Howel ap Oweyn Voyl and the heir of William de Tranemole and the daughter of Geoffrey de Honford hold in Mottrum in *le Haghe* one messuage and one carucate of land by knight service and render yearly 4s.[280]

7.16   Item John de Hyde, knight, holds in the same one messuage and seven acres of land by knight service and renders to the lord 13d. yearly.[281]

7.17   The same John de Hyde holds in the same one plot of land called *le Grenehouse* and renders to the lord for reveyeld yearly 3d. and for warde 1d., and he makes suit to the lord's mill for the same tenement.[282]

7.18   Item Richard de Dewisnape holds one messuage and half of one bovate of land there and renders 5s. 2d. a year and makes suit to the lord's mill.[283]

7.19   Item Ralph de Wolegh holds there one messuage and eight acres of land by the aforesaid services except suit of the mill and renders yearly 3s.[284]

7.20   Item they say that John son of John de Radeclyf holds there one messuage with 1 garden and half a rood of land and renders yearly 1¼d. And he makes suit to the lord's mill.[285]

277 See **3.12**.
278 The aforesaid Richard and William.
279 See **3.13**.
280 See **3.14**.
281 See **3.15**.
282 See **3.18**.
283 See **3.16**.
284 See **3.17**.
285 See **6.02**. It will be noted that the scribe of this draft, having copied from m. 3 from **3.01** (with the exception of the entry on Stayley which has been reserved until later) to **3.17**, now continues from **6.02**, placing the same # mark both between **6.01** and **6.02** and in the margin here as a guide to the succeeding copyist, whether himself or another. The evidence thus indicates that for whatever reason m. 6 was written as it is, it is incomplete and not as intended. Membranes 3 and 6 are both partial and complementary rough drafts, which needed to be combined to

m. 7

7.21 Item W. de Caryngton', Chivaler, tenet | [48] ibidem unam placeam vocatam Harop' per servicium militare et reddit per annum xviij d. et j lb. Cumin. |

Wernyth'
[49] **7.22** Item dicunt quod Ricardus filius Roberti de Eton' qui est etatis quindecim annorum tenet villam | [50] de Wernyth' de domino de Longedendale per servicium militare etcetera.[z]

m. 7d
[Written by hand 2 on upturned membrane, i.e. the other way up from the recto.]

Magna Holyn'
[1] **7.23** Item, dicunt quod J. Holynworth' tenet magnam Holynworth' per servicium militare et reddit per annum iij s. iiij d., et facit *Haghhag* | [2] et opus molendini ut supra, et dat pro Reveyeld' vij d. ob., et pro Ward' ij d. ob. per annum, et facit sectam ad | [3] Curiam de Mottrum et inveniet ij Judices in eadem, et facit sectam ad molendinum domini. |

Parva Holynworth
[4] **7.24** Item, dicunt quod Ricardus de Wolegh' tenet terciam partem de Parva Holyn' et facit sectam ad Curiam predictam et inveniet | [5] j judicem in eadem, et reddit per annum xij d., et dat pro Reveyeld j d. ob. et pro Ward' ob., et facit sectam ad molendinum domini. |
[6] **7.25** Et Cristiana de Holyn tenet duas partes eiusdem ville per servicium militare, et reddit per annum pro eisdem duabus partibus et pro | [7] Thorntley iij s. per annum, et pro Reveyeld xij d. et pro Ward' iiij d., et facit *Haghehag'* et opus molendini ut supra, | [8] et facit sectam ad molendinum domini.
7.26 Item, Philippus de Eggerton' tenet xl acras terre ibidem et reddit per annum ixij d.,[a] et dat[b] pro | [9] Reveyeld xij d. et pro Ward' iiij d., et facit *Hagheh'*, opus molendini et sectam ad molendinum domini[c] ut supra. |

(z) Stitched to the lower left-hand side of m. 7 is a small parchment tag bearing the label: **34 Edw⁰ 3**.
(a) *Sic* for xij d.
(b) *dat* interlineated.
(c) *domini* interlineated.

m. 7

7.21 Item W. de Caryngton, knight, holds there one place called Harop by knight service and renders yearly 18d. and 1 lb. of cumin.[286]

Wernyth (Werneth)
7.22 Item they say that Richard son of Robert de Eton who is fifteen years of age holds the township of Wernyth from the lord of Longdendale by knight service etcetera.[287]
[288]

m. 7d

Great Holyn' (Hollingworth)
7.23 Item, they say that J. Holynworth holds Great Holynworth by knight service and renders yearly 3s. 4d., and does Haghhag and work of the mill as above, and gives for reveyeld 7½d. and for ward 2½d. yearly, and he makes suit to the Court of Mottrum and will find 2 doomsmen in the same, and makes suit to the lord's mill.[289]

Little Holynworth
7.24 Item, they say that Richard de Wolegh holds a third part of Little Holyn' and makes suit to the aforesaid Court and will find 1 doomsman in the same, and renders yearly 12d., and gives for reveyeld 1½d. and for ward ½d. and he makes suit to the lord's mill.[290]
7.25 And Christiana de Holyn holds two parts of the same township by knight service, and renders yearly for the same two parts and for Thorntley 3s. yearly, and for reveyeld 12d. and for ward 4d., and does Haghehag and work of the mill as above, and makes suit to the lord's mill.[291]
7.26 Item, Philip de Eggerton holds 40 acres of land there and renders yearly [12]d., and gives for reveyeld 12d. and for ward 4d., and does Hagheh', work of the mill and suit to the lord's mill as above.[292]

provide all the necessary information. That combination was here taken in hand, and this draft prepares for the extent to be copied from itself and m. 6 as required.

286 See **6.03**.
287 See **6.62**. The scribe here rectifies an error by inserting amongst the major tenants, between Mottram and Hollingworth, the entry on Werneth, which had been appended almost as an afterthought at the end of m. 6. We are asked to point out that the township of Werneth was mistakenly omitted from the map in *Maccl. Acc.*, p. xxii. The *etcetera* indicates that this is a draft only, and one more stage in preparation for a final version of the extent.
288 On a small parchment tag the label **34 Edward 3**.
289 See **6.04**.
290 See **6.05**.
291 See **6.06**, where this last service is given as *drive & lede*. Note the variant spelling of the place-name.
292 See **6.07**.

m. 7d

Stavelegh'[(d)]

[10] **7.27** Item, dicunt quod Robertus de Stavel' tenet Manerium de Stavel'[(e)] de domino de Long' per servicium militare, [[et idem Robertus | [11] habet diem ad ostendendum per que servicia tenet idem manerium.]][(f)]   [(g) (h)]

(d) Below the heading is a marginal note in hand 2: *habet diem de servic'*.
(e) *per* struck through, *de* interlineated.
(f) The clauses *et idem Robertus ... idem manerium* struck through.
(g) At the top of m. 7d the right way up, in a later, possibly seventeenth-century, hand: *Extenta dominii de Longdendale anno xxxiiij° Edwardi tercij.*
(h) On the left-hand edge, vertically, in a nineteenth-century hand: *Extent of the Manor of Longdendale 34 th : ED : 3ᵈ.*

m. 7d

Stavelegh (Stayley)

7.27   Item, they say that Robert de Stavel' holds the manor of Stavel' from the lord of Long' by knight service, [[and the same Robert has a day for showing by what services he holds the same manor.]] [293]   [294]

[293] See **3.04**. The last clause is here struck through.

[294] Further information relevant to the Extent of Longdendale is to be found in the unfortunately defective Inquisition Post Mortem of Isabel de Stokeport, 1370 (CHES 3/6, 28), which states *inter alia* that Isabella, daughter and heiress of Richard de Stokeport, knight, held a piece of land with appurtenances in Hattersley of the earl of Chester as parcel of his lordship of Longdendale by the services of ploughing each year (with her own animals) in Lent at the manor of Tintwistle, in the demesne lands there, taking daily for the sustenance of those working each plough [.....] oat cakes [......] one gallon of ale and three herrings, and suit at the court of Tintwistle [........] and by making Ha[..]werk for the lord's fawning, that is across beyond the Crowdenes (*pro feonacione domini, videlicet extransversum le Crowdenes*) at the lord's will once a year.

   This Isabel de Stokeport, who died on the feast of St Luke the Evangelist, 43 Edward III (18 October 1369), was the daughter of the Richard de Eton mentioned in **3.12**, **6.62**, **7.12** and **7.22**, who was there described as aged 15. See Earwaker, ii. 269. The description of the services by which she held part of Hattersley may be compared with the statements concerning Richard de Eton's holding in **3.12** and **7.12**. That concerning the 'sustenance of those working each plough' is most fully detailed in **3.05**, though the details there differ slightly. The *Ha*.[..]*werk* referred to appears to be essentially identical with the *Haghehag* mentioned several times in the extent and defined in **3.08**. The use of the word *feonacione* 'fawning' here clearly indicates the purpose of the service in the management of the herds of deer in the breeding season, and supports our translation of *venacione* in **3.08** as 'venison' rather than 'hunting'. It is interesting, however, that the location of the service in this case should be so explicitly identified as being on the other side of Crowden, since it seems likely that similar service by others mentioned in these membranes may have been rendered at the deer hay on the Hague in Mottram mentioned in note 53 above. Crowden (well-known to walkers on the Pennine Way) is situated approximately four miles E.N.E. of Tintwistle, and Hey, Hey Edge, Hey Moss and Hey Clough are all marked on O.S. maps to the N.E. of Crowden.

APPENDIX

LONGDENDALE TENANCIES

In the following table all the tenancies under the lordship of Longdendale mentioned in SC 11/897 *are summarised, together with the rents, works and services by which they were held, with the evidence provided by the different membranes. After the first two entries they are listed under manors, mainly following the order in the descriptive membranes 3, 6 and 7, with the parallel entries in membranes 4 and 5 alongside, followed at the end by those entries in mm. 4 and 5 where any parallels are uncertain. Entry numbers and rents are printed bold, as are statements that tenements are in decay. Where the substance in mm. 4 or 5 differs significantly from the listing in mm. 3/6 and 7, those details are shaded.*

For economy of space, numerous symbols and abbreviations are used, a key to which is provided at the foot of each page.

Membranes 3, 6 & 7	Membrane 4	Membrane 5
3.02, **7.02** Buckton Castle ruined, of no value.		
3.03, **7.02b** Hall chamber and chapel, 'let at farm as below'. [*Possibly Arnfield, see nn. 40, 43.*]		
Stayley		
3.04, **7.27** Robert de Stavelegh, manor of Stayley, ks, 'has a day'.		**5.53** 'various rents & works' **13s. 1d.**

Key to symbols: adj adjacent; acr acre(s); ap appurtenances; b burgage; bs burgages; c croft; ct curtilage; dm provision of doomsman/men (with number supplied in brackets); dr daughter; etm earthwork at Tintwistle mill; gdn garden; gr grange; hh 'haghehag'; jr junior; ks knight service; ld land; mes messuage; mw meadow; pol parcel of land; ps ploughing service; r revegeld; rd rood; rs reaping service; rw revegeld & ward combined; sc suit of Mottram court; sm suit of the lord's mill; t toft; w ward; yoa years of age.

Membranes 3, 6 & 7	Membrane 4	Membrane 5

Newton

3.05, **7.03** Robert de
Newton, manor of
Newton, ks, rs, ps.

5.54 for ps & rs
11s. 1d.

Matley

3.06, **7.04** *properly* John
son of Wm de Hyde,
½ manor of Matley,
in fact Sir John de Hyde,
r **3d.** w **1d.**

4.67 from ld of William
de Mattelegh, **2s. 4d.**

3.07, **7.05** John de Hyde,
¼ manor of Matley, ks.

4.66 from ld of John
de Hyde, **1s. 8d.**

3.08, **7.06** Henry son of
Robert de Holynworth,
¼ manor of Matley, ks, hh,
etm, 2dm, **4s.**

4.68 John de Hyde, for ld
of wardship of the son of
Robert de Holynworth, **6s.**

5.51 from Matley,
4s.

Godley

3.09, **7.07** John de Hyde,
½ manor of Godley, ks, **1d.**
3.09, **7.08** Howel ap
Oweyn & son of Wm
Tranemell, ¼ Godley, ks.
3.09, **7.09** dr of Geoffrey
de Honford, (4 yoa)
¼ Godley, ks.
3.10, **7.10** Robert le Ward
de Godlegh, ½ carucate
+ 1 mes, hh, etm.

5.52 from
Godley, **2d.**

Key to symbols: adj adjacent; acr acre(s); ap appurtenances; b burgage; bs burgages;
c croft; ct curtilage; dm provision of doomsman/men (with number supplied in brackets);
dr daughter; etm earthwork at Tintwistle mill; gdn garden; gr grange; hh 'haghehag';
jr junior; ks knight service; ld land; mes messuage; mw meadow; pol parcel of land;
ps ploughing service; r revegeld; rd rood; rs reaping service; rw revegeld & ward combined;
sc suit of Mottram court; sm suit of the lord's mill; t toft; w ward; yoa years of age.

Membranes 3, 6 & 7	**Membrane 4**	**Membrane 5**
3.11, **7.11** John son of John de Godlegh, 1 mes + 24 acr, **1d.**		[*See* **5.52** *above.*]

Hattersley

3.12, **7.12** Richard de Eton (15 yoa), ½ manor of Hattersley, ks, ps, rs, hh, etm. **3.13**, **7.13-14** Wm Caryngton, kt, ½ manor of Hattersley, same services 1 dm, rw, **9d.** **7.13** adds sm, sc.		**5.55-57** services **3s.**

Mottram

3.14, **7.15** John de Hyde, Howel ap Oweyn, son of Wm Tranemol, dr of Geoffrey de Honford, in *le Haghe*, 1 mes & 1 carucate, ks, **4s.**		**5.47** from land of Wm Bagylegh in *le haghe*, **4s.**
3.15, **7.16** John de Hyde, 1 mes & 7 acr, ks, **1s. 1d.**	**4.08** Henry Gybon part of John de Hyde's ld, **6½d.**	**5.50** John de Hyde ld in Mottram, **1s. 1d.**
3.16, **7.18** Richard de Diewysnape, 1 mes, ½ bovate, **5s. 2d.** **7.18** adds sm.	**4.10** Richard de Dewysnape **2s. 6d.** **4.11** rw **1½d.**	**5.49** Richard de Dewsnape, **5s. 2d.**
3.17, **7.19** Ralph de Wolegh, 1 mes & 8 acr, same services except sm, **3s.**	**4.58** Ralph Tillessone, (ld unspecified) **1s. 6d.**	**5.48** Ralph de Wolegh *Brodlathum*, **3s.**

Key to symbols: adj adjacent; acr acre(s); ap appurtenances; b burgage; bs burgages; c croft; ct curtilage; dm provision of doomsman/men (with number supplied in brackets); dr daughter; etm earthwork at Tintwistle mill; gdn garden; gr grange; hh 'haghehag'; jr junior; ks knight service; ld land; mes messuage; mw meadow; pol parcel of land; ps ploughing service; r revegeld; rd rood; rs reaping service; rw revegeld & ward combined; sc suit of Mottram court; sm suit of the lord's mill; t toft; w ward; yoa years of age.

Membranes 3, 6 & 7	**Membrane 4**	**Membrane 5**

3.18, **7.17** John de Hyde, *le Grenehouse*, r **3d.**, w **1d.** **7.17** adds sm.

4.09 Henry Gybon rw **1½d.**

6.02, **7.20** John son of John de Radeclyft, 1 mes, gdn & ½ rd, **1¼d.** **7.20** adds sm.

6.03, **7.21** Wm de Caryngton, *Harop*, ks, **1s. 6d.** + 1 lb. cumin.

Mottram continued (**6.48–6.60** brought forward from after Tintwistle in the ms)

6.48 Adam de Harop, 1 mes & land adj, **4s. 3d.**
6.49 Stephen de Harop jr, 1 mes & land adj, **4s. 3d.** rw **1¼d.**

4.16 Adam de Harap **2s. 1½d.**
4.17 Stephen his bro **2s. 1½d.**
4.18 their rw **¾d.**

5.35 Stephen & Adam de Harap, **7s.**

6.50 Henry Gybon, 1 mes & land adj, **3s.**, rw **4d.**

4.06–07 Henry Gybon, **1s. 6d.**, rw **2½d.**

5.30 Henry Gybon, **3s.**

6.51 Jordan del Haghe, 1 mes & land adj, **4s. 9d.**, rw **4d.**

4.12–13 Jordan del Haghe, **2s. 4½d.**, rw **2½d.**

5.32 Jordan del Hagh, **4s. 9d.**

6.52 Stephen de Harop sr, 1 mes & land adj, **4s.**

4.02 Stephen de Harap, **2s.**

5.29 Stephen de Harap, *le holehous* **4s.**

6.53 Watkyn Rowessone, 1 mes & land adj, **6s. 3d.**, rw **4d.**

4.19–20 Wadkyn del Haghe **3s. 1½d.** rw **2½d.**

5.33 Walter son of Ralph **7s.**

Key to symbols: adj adjacent; acr acre(s); ap appurtenances; b burgage; bs burgages; c croft; ct curtilage; dm provision of doomsman/men (with number supplied in brackets); dr daughter; etm earthwork at Tintwistle mill; gdn garden; gr grange; hh 'haghehag'; jr junior; ks knight service; ld land; mes messuage; mw meadow; pol parcel of land; ps ploughing service; r revegeld; rd rood; rs reaping service; rw revegeld & ward combined; sc suit of Mottram court; sm suit of the lord's mill; t toft; w ward; yoa years of age.

Membranes 3, 6 & 7	**Membrane 4**	**Membrane 5**
6.54 Wm del Wharell, 1 mes & land adj, **2s. 10d.**, rw **2½d.**	**4.22–23** Wm de Wharell, **1s. 5d.** rw **1½d.**	**5.31** Wm del Wharell, **7s.**
6.55 Wm son of John, 1 mes & land adj, **9s. 2d.**, rw **4d.**	**4.14–15** Wm de Godelegh, **4s. 7d.** rw **2½d.**	**5.20** land of John de Godelegh, **11s. 4d.**
6.56 Ralph Tyllessone, (*Thomerode*) **2s.**	**4.59** Ralph Tillessone, **1s.**	
6.57 Roger del Bothum, 1 mes & land adj, **4s.**	**4.24** Roger de Bothum, from Mottram, **2s.**	
6.58–59 Hugh del Ruggeway, 1 mes & land adj, **14s.**, rw **3¼d.**	**4.04** Richard del Riggeway, **7s.** rw **1½d.**	**5.34** Ric de Ruggeway, **14s.**
6.60 Thomas Foucher, Little Rudyng, **2s.**	**4.21** Thomas Foucher, **1s.**	

Hollingworth

6.04, **7.23** John de Holynworth, Great Holynworth, ks, **3s. 4d.**, hh, etm, r **7½d.**, w **2½d.**, 1dm, sc. **7.23** has 2dm, and adds sm.		**5.43** John de Holynworth, **3s. 4d.**
6.05, **7.24** Richard de Wolegh, 1/3 Little Holynworth, sc, 1dm, **1s.**, r **1½d.**, w **½d.** **7.24** adds sm.	**4.61** Richard de Wolegh, free rent, **6d.** **4.62** r **¾d.**	**5.46** Richard de Wolegh, **1s.**

Key to symbols: adj adjacent; acr acre(s); ap appurtenances; b burgage; bs burgages; c croft; ct curtilage; dm provision of doomsman/men (with number supplied in brackets); dr daughter; etm earthwork at Tintwistle mill; gdn garden; gr grange; hh 'haghehag'; jr junior; ks knight service; ld land; mes messuage; mw meadow; pol parcel of land; ps ploughing service; r revegeld; rd rood; rs reaping service; rw revegeld & ward combined; sc suit of Mottram court; sm suit of the lord's mill; t toft; w ward; yoa years of age.

Membranes 3, 6 & 7	Membrane 4	Membrane 5
6.06, **7.25** Christiana de Holyn, 2/3 Little Holynworth, and Thorntelegh, ks, **3s.**, r **1s.**, w **4d.**, hh, etm, **7.25** adds sm.	**4.70** Christiana de Holynworth, rent, **1s. 6d.** **4.71** (Wm her son) **1½d.** **4.72** r **4½d.**	**5.45** Christiana de Holynworth, **3s.**
6.07, **7.26** Philip de Eggerton, 40 acr, **1s.**, r **1s.**, w **4d.**, hh, etm, **7.26** adds sm.	[*See **4.56** below, p. 82.*]	**5.59** del *Oldefeld* in Holynworth, **1s.**

Tintwistle

Membranes 3, 6 & 7	Membrane 4	Membrane 5
6.09 Roger de Bothum, 1 b, **1s.**	**4.30** Wm his son, **6d.**	[*? Wm le Hune'*, ***5.11***]
6.10 Robert de Dewysnape, 1 b, **1s.**	**4.46** Robert Dewysnape 3 b, **9½d.** [*Includes **6.18, 6.20** below.*]	**5.13** Robert de Dewysnape 1 b, **1s.**
6.11 John le Tieu, 1 b, **10d.**	[*See **4.49** below.*]	[*? See **5.14** below.*]
6.12 Wm Nyksone, 1 gr, 1 ct, **4d.** **6.13** Wm Nyksone, 1 t, **2d.**		[*? Wm le Hune'* ***5.11***]
6.14 Thomas le Barker, 1 b, **1s.**	**4.32** Thomas le Barker, 1 b, **6d.**	**5.09** Thomas le Barker, **1s.**
6.15 John son of Thomas le Forster, 1 little house upon *le Syk*, **6d.**		
6.16 Magot Dok's wife, 3 b, **2s.**	**4.41** Magot wife of Robert Dokeson, **2s. 3d.** [*Includes **6.22–23, 6.26** below.*]	**5.05** Mag Dok's dr, **2s.**

Key to symbols: adj adjacent; acr acre(s); ap appurtenances; b burgage; bs burgages; c croft; ct curtilage; dm provision of doomsman/men (with number supplied in brackets); dr daughter; etm earthwork at Tintwistle mill; gdn garden; gr grange; hh 'haghehag'; jr junior; ks knight service; ld land; mes messuage; mw meadow; pol parcel of land; ps ploughing service; r revegeld; rd rood; rs reaping service; rw revegeld & ward combined; sc suit of Mottram court; sm suit of the lord's mill; t toft; w ward; yoa years of age.

Membranes 3, 6 & 7	**Membrane 4**	**Membrane 5**
6.17 Thomas le Barker, 1 b, (ex Cobbok's) **1s.**	**4.44** Thomas le Barker, **3½d.**	
6.18 Robert de Dewysnape, 1 t, **4d.**	**4.46** (*See 6.10 above.*)	
6.19 Wm Geffrou, 1 b & land adj, **2s.**	**4.48** Wm Geffreu, **1s.**	**5.24** Wm Geffreu, for 1 acre, **1s.**
6.20 Robert de Dewysnape, 1 pol, **3d.**	**4.46** (*See 6.10 above.*)	
6.21 *le Herstoncloghouses* & 6 acr, used to render **4s.** now **in decay**.		**5.25** Wm Geffrou, *herstancloghous*, **1s.**
6.22 Magot Dok's wife, 1 c, **6d.**	**4.41** (*as above*)	
6.23 Same Magot, 1 t, **6d.**	**4.41** (*as above*)	
6.24 Robert Dok's son, 1 t, **6d.**	**4.42** Robert Dokeson, **3d.**	
6.25 Nicholas son of Wm son of Thomas, 2 b, 3 t, 1 c, **3s. 10d.**		**5.06** Nicholas son of Wm, bs, **3s. 10d.**
6.26 Magot Dok's wife, 1 b, **1s.**	**4.41** (*as above*)	**5.07** Mag Dok's dr, **1s.**
6.27 Henry le Wylde, 1 b (wife's), & 1 t, **1s. 9d.**	**4.35** Henry le Wylde, 1 b, **10½d.**	**5.08** Henry le Wylde, b only, **1s.**
6.28 Henry le Smyth of Stokport, 1 mes & forge, **6d.**	**4.40** Thomas the Smith, **3d.**	

Key to symbols: adj adjacent; acr acre(s); ap appurtenances; b burgage; bs burgages; c croft; ct curtilage; dm provision of doomsman/men (with number supplied in brackets); dr daughter; etm earthwork at Tintwistle mill; gdn garden; gr grange; hh 'haghehag'; jr junior; ks knight service; ld land; mes messuage; mw meadow; pol parcel of land; ps ploughing service; r revegeld; rd rood; rs reaping service; rw revegeld & ward combined; sc suit of Mottram court; sm suit of the lord's mill; t toft; w ward; yoa years of age.

Membranes 3, 6 & 7	**Membrane 4**	**Membrane 5**
6.29 Henry le Wyld, 1 b & *le Rodefeld*, **8s. 6d.**	**4.36** Henry le Wyld, ld in *Rodefeld*, **4s. 3d.**	**5.03** Henry le Wylde, *Rodefeld*, **8s. 6d.**
6.30 1 mes on *le Syk*, ex Robert le Smyth, **7d.**		**5.16** b Robert le Smyth elder's **7d.**
6.31 1 pol & ct, ex Symon le Smith **in decay**, used to render **9d.**		**5.17** from Symon the smith's forge **7d.**
6.32 John son of Wm de Hyde, 6 b & 9 acr, **14s. 5d.** **6.33** Same John, 1 pol next to mill used to render **6d.**	**4.43** John de Hyde, ld, **14s. 5d.** [? **4.57** *below* ?]	**5.12** John de Hyde, bs, **14s. 5d.** (*levab'*)
6.34 John Hobrode, 1 b & 1 t, **1s. 4d.**	**4.34** John Hobrode, 1 b, **8d.**	**5.10** John Hobrod, *burg'*, **1s. 4d.**
6.35 Robert de Dewysnape, 1 b & lands adj, **8s.**	**4.69** Robert de Deuwesnape rent **4s.**	**5.19** R. de Dewsnape *aspenforlong* **8s.**
6.36 1 b, ex Robert le Merser **in decay**, used to render **1s.**		
6.37 1 b, ex Wm le Stiwardessone, **in decay**, used to render **1s.**		[*See* **5.15** *below.*]
6.38 Richard de Halghton, *le Wallefeld*, **9s.**	**4.39** Richard de Halghton, for his ld, **4s. 6d.**	**5.04** R. de Halghton, *le Wallefeld*, **9s.**
6.39 John Hobberode, *le Wallecroft*, **3s.** **6.40** Same John & Thomas le Barker, 1 pol, **10s.**	**4.33** John Hobrode, **3s. 7d.** **4.31** Thomas le Barker, **3s. 7d.**	

Key to symbols: adj adjacent; acr acre(s); ap appurtenances; b burgage; bs burgages; c croft; ct curtilage; dm provision of doomsman/men (with number supplied in brackets); dr daughter; etm earthwork at Tintwistle mill; gdn garden; gr grange; hh 'haghehag'; jr junior; ks knight service; ld land; mes messuage; mw meadow; pol parcel of land; ps ploughing service; r revegeld; rd rood; rs reaping service; rw revegeld & ward combined; sc suit of Mottram court; sm suit of the lord's mill; t toft; w ward; yoa years of age.

Membranes 3, 6 & 7	Membrane 4	Membrane 5
6.41 Wm de Thornley, 1 b & lands adj, **14s. 6d.**	**4.45** Wm de Thorntelegh, **7s. 3d.**	**5.18** Wm de Thorntelegh, **14s. 3d.**
6.42 *le Heewodeheyghe* is accustomed to render **12s.**	**4.37** (?) Robert Godard, **6s.**	**5.21** *Ewodeheye*, **12s.**
6.43 John le Tieu, 1 mw, **1s. 2d.**	[*See* **4.49** *below*.]	[*See* **5.14** *below*.]
6.44 Wm le Mulner, 2 mes & land adj, **11s.**	**4.27** Wm le Mulnere, **5s. 6d.**	**5.23** Wm le Mulner, **11s.**

Arnfield

6.45 Roger del Bothum, Parva Arnefeld, **£1**, rw **4d.**	**4.28** Roger de Bothum, Arnwayfeld,	**5.22** R. de Bothum, Arnewayfeld,
6.46 Same Roger, Magna Arnefeld, **£1 6s.**, rw **8d.**	**£1 3s.**	**£2 6s.**
	4.29 rw **7½d.**	

Micklehurst and Littlehurst

6.47 John Lastles, Simon le Muleward, William del Fernylegh, Adam de Gaunt, & Thomas le Prestessone, Mukelhurst & Lytelhurst, **6½ marks = £4 6s. 8d.**	**4.54** S. the miller **10s. 11½d.** **4.51** Wm Symeson **10s. 11d.** **4.50** A. de Gaunt **11s. 11½d.** **4.52** Th. son of Richard the chaplain, **10s. 5½d.** [= *£2 4s.3½d.*]	**5.38** tenants of Mukklehurst & Litelhurst, **£4 6s. 8d.**

Werneth

6.62, 7.22 Richard, son of Robert de Eton, 15 yoa, Wernyth, ks.

Key to symbols: adj adjacent; acr acre(s); ap appurtenances; b burgage; bs burgages; c croft; ct curtilage; dm provision of doomsman/men (with number supplied in brackets); dr daughter; etm earthwork at Tintwistle mill; gdn garden; gr grange; hh 'haghehag'; jr junior; ks knight service; ld land; mes messuage; mw meadow; pol parcel of land; ps ploughing service; r revegeld; rd rood; rs reaping service; rw revegeld & ward combined; sc suit of Mottram court; sm suit of the lord's mill; t toft; w ward; yoa years of age.

Membranes 3, 6 & 7	Membrane 4	Membrane 5
Revegeld		
		5.58 Revegeld from whole of lordship, **10s.**
Herbage/Agistment		
6.63 Longeden', leased at fixed rent from Martinmas 1359 until the same feast 1360, for **£12.**		**5.39–40** Tenants of Longdend[...] herbage **£12.**
Mill		
		5.41 Mill & Stallage **£4.**
Fishery		
6.65 Fishery of Edrowe farmed to Peter de Arden, Michaelmas 1359 until the same feast next following, **6s. 8d.**		

Tenancies referred to in membranes 4 and 5 but not described in mm. 3/6 or 7:

	Membrane 4	Membrane 5
Mottram		
	4.03 Stephen de Harap sr, land in *le Haghe* **2d.** *[Can this be 6.02?]*	
		5.36 Adam le Tayllour, **in decay, 10s. 1d.**

Key to symbols: adj adjacent; acr acre(s); ap appurtenances; b burgage; bs burgages; c croft; ct curtilage; dm provision of doomsman/men (with number supplied in brackets); dr daughter; etm earthwork at Tintwistle mill; gdn garden; gr grange; hh 'haghehag'; jr junior; ks knight service; ld land; mes messuage; mw meadow; pol parcel of land; ps ploughing service; r revegeld; rd rood; rs reaping service; rw revegeld & ward combined; sc suit of Mottram court; sm suit of the lord's mill; t toft; w ward; yoa years of age.

	Membrane 4	**Membrane 5**

Tintwistle

4.38 Richard Halghton,
bs, **1s. 11d.**
[*Presumably at least two,
and probably four bs.*]

4.47 Robert Dewysnape,
land unspecified, **8d.**

4.49 John son of John de
Dewysnape, land
unspecified,   **5d.**
[*This equals half year's
rent of John le Tieu's 6.11.*]

5.14 John son of
John de Dewsnape,
b,   **1s.**
[*Could be a different b.*]

5.11 Wm le Hune',
for b(s), **1s. 4d.**
[*Presumably 2 bs.*]
? *Possibly Wm
Nykson 6.12–13,
or Wm son of Roger
de Bothum 4.30.*]

5.15 Robert le Smyth,
b, **1s.**
[*Possibly 6.37 above.*]

Hollingworth

4.56 Robert de Holynworth,
land unspecified, **6d.**
[*Can this be Oldefeld
6.07, 7.26, and 5.59, p. 77 above?*]

4.57 Robert de Holynworth,
pol next to the mill, **1d.**
[*Can this be 6.33, p. 79 above?*]

Key to symbols: adj adjacent; acr acre(s); ap appurtenances; b burgage; bs burgages;
c croft; ct curtilage; dm provision of doomsman/men (with number supplied in brackets);
dr daughter; etm earthwork at Tintwistle mill; gdn garden; gr grange; hh 'haghehag';
jr junior; ks knight service; ld land; mes messuage; mw meadow; pol parcel of land;
ps ploughing service; r revegeld; rd rood; rs reaping service; rw revegeld & ward combined;
sc suit of Mottram court; sm suit of the lord's mill; t toft; w ward; yoa years of age.

PROSOPOGRAPHICAL INDEX

In the following Index all persons named in the membranes of SC 11/897 *are listed, and everything there recorded about them is gathered together, along with some information from other sources. (Membrane 1 is simply a list of names with no additional information, though it may indeed be a list of trespassers in Longdendale water.) Persons are listed in alphabetical order, together with the entry number(s) where they appear. For the benefit of students of family history, all the variant spellings of persons' surnames which appear in the membranes are listed and referenced. It should be noted that when people are identified by their relationship, i.e. as son, daughter, wife of an individual named by Christian name only, e.g.* Willelmus filius Johannis, *that would probably have been spoken in English as* William John's son, *which would later appear as the surname* Johnson. *For that reason such cases have been listed below under the patronymic. Latin Christian names are generally translated. Other sources frequently referred to include the* 1408 Rental of Longdendale (MS Harl. 2039, f. 113) *cited as* 1408 Rental, *and* County Court of Chester Indictments Roll, 1354–77 (CHES 25/4), m. 29, *cited as* CCCIR 1373, *a transcript of relevant parts of which was kindly supplied by the late Mrs Phyllis Hill of the Ranulf Higden Society.*

Adam, Thomas son of   **1.17**

Adam, [......] of   **1.19**

Arden, Peter de   **6.65**
Holder of the lease or farm of the fishery of Etherow, from *Rontandebrok* to Salter's Brook, from Michaelmas 1359 to Michaelmas 1360 for 6s. 8d. The accounts for the following year indicate that the lease was not then renewed, 'for lack of a farmer'. See Table 1, p. xxxviii above, with note on p. xlii.

Bagylegh, William de   **5.47**
Referred to just once among free tenants in Longdendale as the former holder of land in Mottram in *le Haghe*, for which 4s. was paid. Presumably William de Baggilegh the younger, who was son of William de Baggilegh, knight, of Baguley near Northenden. He became lord of the manor of Godley after 1319, and held it until his death, when the Baggilegh estates seem to have been divided between his two sisters, one of whom was married to John de Hyde. It is not clear exactly what happened to the Baguley estates about this period: see Earwaker, ii. 156–7. This land in *le Haghe* appears, however, to be that referred to in **3.14** and **7.15** as held jointly by **John de Hyde, knight, Howel ap Oweyn**, the son of **William de Tranemol** and the daughter and heiress of **Geoffrey de Honford**, which yielded 4s. a year.

Barker, Thomas le   **4.31–32**; **4.44**; **5.09**; **6.14**; **6.17**; **6.40**
Holder (**6.14** with **4.32** and **5.09**) of a burgage in Tintwistle rendering 12d. a year.

Holder at will jointly with **John Hobberode** (**6.40**) of a plot of land in Tintwistle rendering 10s. a year. **4.31** may represent his share of the rent for this property. In **4.44** paid 3½d. for unspecified land. His occupational name indicates involvement with tanning. In the 1408 Rental the wife of Tho le barker paid 4s. 6¾d. as a tenant at will in Tintwistle.

Benfort (or **Beufort**), [...] son of Peter de   1.37

Bentelegh, John de   1.16

Botelir (Butler), **Adam le**   1.05

Bothum, Roger del   3.01; 4.24; 4.28–29; 5.22; 6.01; 6.09; 6.45–46; 6.57; [7.01]
One of the jurors of **3.01**, **6.01** (in lacuna in **7.01**). From **6.45–46** with **4.28–29** it is clear that he held at will Great and Little Arnfield, rendering for Great Arnfield 26s. + 8d. for reveyeld and ward, and for Little Arnfield 20s. + 4d for reveyeld and ward; from **6.57** with **4.24** that he held at will a messuage and land adjacent in Mottram rendering 4s., and from **6.09** that he held a burgage in Tintwistle rendering 12d. for which his son **William** pays the Martinmas rent in **4.30**. It appears from CCCIR 1373 that **Sir William Caryngton**, then farmer of the lordship of Longdendale, between the years 1361 and 1373 demolished *inter alia* a messuage in Arnfield worth 20s. that was Roger del Bothum's.

Bothum, William son of Roger del   4.30
This entry records his Martinmas payment of 6d. for one burgage, probably the one held by his father in **6.09**. The possibility needs to be considered that he may have been the person named **William le Hune** (or **Hund'**) in **5.17**. In the 1408 Rental a William del Bothum paid 5s. ¼d. as a tenant at will in Tintwistle.

Botiller, Willeam de, de Wemme le puisne   m. 3, left margin
Name found in the first and only line of the incomplete charter or similar record for which m. 3 had originally been used in landscape format before being re-used in vertical format as the first membrane of the draft of the 1360 extent.

Brok(e), [....] son of   **1.21**, and
[....] his son   **1.22**

Brunham, (or **Burnham**), **Master John de, the younger**   6.01
Chamberlain of Chester, one of the officials before whom the extent was made. See *ChAcc2*, pp. 124–6.

Byrch, Richard de   5.64
Referred to once at the end of m. 5d in a short section which may imply that his goods had been forfeited to the lord for some reason. A Richard Byrches was fined in Shareshull's sessions (1353), of which 26s. 8d. was payable to the poker of

Macclesfield, 1354–55 (SC 6/802/11, m. 2) and it is possible that these entries in **5.64** relate to that fine. In the Longdendale Accounts for 1358–59 (SC 6/802/15, m. 1) the herbage, focage and arable of Longdendale are recorded as having been farmed by the steward to Richard del Byrches, Henry Erneshagh and others for £12. He does not appear again in the accounts in that capacity, but in the bailiff's account of March 1366–March 1367 (SC 6/803/13, m. 3) Richard de Byrches appears as 'deputy of the same Adam in the lordship' (i.e. Adam de Kyngeslegh, the then bailiff) exercising responsibility for the wholesale sale of the issues of the mill, and also as the recipient of an allowance of £1 10s. 5d. as 'keeper of the lord's wood there'. In the 1367–68 account (SC 6/803/13, m. 4) the keeper of the wood (unnamed) received £1. In view of the references to corn and the mill it is also possible that this section at the end of m. 5 might relate to and postdate his role in 1367, though it is clearly a postscript added after the main body of the extent.

Caryngton, William de (knight)   3.13; **6.03**; **7.13–14**; **7.21**
(Caryngton **3.13**, **6.03**, **7.21**; Carington **7.13**)
Sir William de Caryngton, whose surname presumably derives from Carrington on the Mersey, west of Sale, in **3.13** and **7.13–14** holds half the manor of Hattersley by the same services as those listed for **Richard de Eton**, viz. knight service, reaping, ploughing, 3 days' 'haghehag', works of the mill, finding one doomsman, suit of the mill, suit of Mottram court, and a share of 9d. reveyeld and ward. In **6.03** and **7.21** he holds a place called Harop (presumably at or near Harrop Edge) in Mottram by knight service and renders 18d. a year and 1lb. of cumin. There is no record of any such payment in m. 4 or m. 5. For Sir William's later tenure of the whole lordship of Longdendale see Introduction, pp. xxiiif., *ChAcc2*, pp. 126–7, and Nevell & Walker, p. 51. In CCCIR 1373 presentments were made against Sir William de Caryngton, then farmer of the lordship of Longdendale, not only for hunting *ad lib.*, but also for widespread demolition between 1361 and 1373 (i.e. throughout his tenure), including *inter alia* a hall, chamber, kitchen and shippon in Longdendale worth 50s. each; a chapel in Tintwistle worth 40s.; a hall and chamber in Tintwistle formerly **William de Hyde's** worth £10; messuages worth 20s. each which were **Richard de Riggesway's**, Richard Dyson's and **William de Godlye's** in Mottram, Henry de Lauton's in Littlehurst and **Roger del Bothum's** in Arnfield; and for the felling and disposal of oaks, ashes and birches to a combined value of £1 18s. 8d. (This was an indictment only, not the outcome of the case.) In the 1408 Rental Sir George de Caryngton paid 6¼d. for Woley as a free tenant + 1¼d. for ward and reveyeld, and 2s. 3¼d. for ward, reveyeld, harvest works and *Grynge* as a free tenant in Hattersley.

Chester, earl of (i.e. Edward the Black Prince)   6.01
Gave instruction for the taking of the extent of the lordship of Longdendale in January 1360.

Cnangreve, John de   1.25

Cobbok   **6.17**
Referred to once as the former tenant of a burgage in Tintwistle now held at will
by **Thomas le Barker**.

Cok(e), Robert son of   **1.07**

Cyntyll, [....] le mulner de   **1.36**

Delves, John de   **6.01**; **[7.01]**
Lieutenant of the Justiciar of Chester, one of the officials before whom the extent
was made. See *ChAcc2*, pp. 123–37.

Dewisnape, Richard de   **3.01**; **3.16**; **4.10–11**; **5.49**; **6.01**; **[7.01]**; **7.18**
(Diewysnape **3.16**, Dewysnape **4.10**, Dewsnape **5.49**, Dewisnape **6.01**, **[7.01]**, **7.18**)
One of the jurors of **3.01**, **6.01** [and **7.01**]. In **3.16** and **7.18** with **5.49** and possibly
also **4.10–11** free tenant of a messuage and half a bovate of land in Mottram for
5s. 2d. + suit of the mill. (N.B. **4.11** records receipt of 1½d. reveyeld and ward
while **3.16** & **7.18** make no mention of reveyeld and ward, but **7.18** mentions suit
of the mill.) His name may be from either Dewsnap in Hollingworth (Dodgson,
i. 310) or the Dewsnap in Tintwistle (*ibid*. p. 327).

Dewysnape, John son of John de   **4.49**; **5.14**
(Dewysnape **4.49**, Dewsnape **5.14**)
In **4.49** renders a Martinmas term rent of 5d. only, but in **5.14** the usual annual
12d. for a burgage in Tintwistle. A burgage is not listed with this tenant's name
in m. 6, and this is likely to be a later tenancy. The 5d. would be an appropriate
half-yearly rent for the burgage which was **John le Tieu**'s in **6.11** but could
equally be for another burgage for less than half a year.

Dewysnape, Robert de   **4.46–47**; **4.69**; **5.13**; **5.19**; **6.08**; **6.10**; **6.18**; **6.20**; **6.35**
(Dewysnape **4.46**, **6.08**, **6.10**, **6.18**, **6.20**; **6.35**, Deuwesnape **4.69**, Dewsnape **5.13**,
5.19)
One of the jurors of **6.08**. From **6.35** with **4.69** and **5.19** it is clear that he held in
Tintwistle for 8s. a burgage with land adjacent called *Aspenforlong*, and from **6.10**
with **5.13** that he also held another burgage there for 12d. **6.18** refers to a toft
which he held in fee for 4d., and **6.20** to another parcel of land in fee held for 3d.
It may be these last three holdings that are referred to in **4.46** where Martinmas
term receipt of 9½d. for three burgages is recorded. **4.47** lists receipt of another
unspecified 8d., which may represent a later tenancy. In the 1408 Rental a Roger
Scott paid 2s. 6¼d. as a tenant at will for *le aspinforlonge*.

Dok, the family of:
The entries for this family illuminate the different stages found in the membranes,
first m. 6, then m. 4, and finally m. 5. See Introduction and Appendix, pp. xviii,
xx, xxxiii, 77f. Regarding the form of the name, which appears only in the genitive

case **Doke** in these manuscripts, note that from the English noun 'priest' we have *Prestessone* (**6.47**), and from the monosyllabic names Til and Ralph/Roe/Rowe we have *Tillessone/ Tyllessone* (**4.59** and **6.56**) and *Rowessone* (**6.53**).

Dok, Mag' daughter of   5.05; **5.07**
In **5.05** pays 2s. annual rent which appears to be for the three burgages in Tintwistle held at will by **Magot wife of Dok** in **6.16**; and in **5.07** another 12d. for a burgage, presumably that also held by the same Magot in **6.26**.

Dok, Magot, wife of   6.16; **6.22–23**; **6.26**; **6.26b**
(Magot' **6.16**, **6.22**, **6.23**, **6.26**, Mag' **6.26b**)
In **6.16** holds at will three burgages for 2s., in **6.22** a croft for 6d., in **6.23** a toft in fee for 6d., in **6.26** a burgage for 12d., and in **6.26b** deleted 'because below' holds *le Smolterhouses* which belonged to **John son of William de Hyde** and renders yearly 12d. This place-name with its possibly local variant pronunciation of 'Smelterhouses' provides early evidence of metal-smelting in Tintwistle.

Dok, Robert, son of   4.42; **6.24**
(Robertus Dokeson **4.41**, **4.42**, filius Doke **6.24**)
In **6.24** holder in fee for 6d. of what is there called a toft, while **4.42** records a half year's rent of 3d. for a burgage. In the 1408 Rental mention is made of a Robert Dooke (perhaps Randle Holme's mistranscription of Docke) the elder, and a Robert his son.

Dokeson, Magot wife of Robert   4.41
Recorded under Martinmas term in Tintwistle as paying 2s. 3d., which seems to imply annual rents of 4s. 6d., presumably for the properties listed in m. 6 as held by **Magot Dok's wife**, with the possible exception of either croft or toft, or with some other adjustment.

Dounes, Edmund de   2d3
Appears here among the Foresters of Macclesfield. He had received his father's forestership in Macclesfield in 1344 (*C.P.R. 1343–45*, p. 355).

Edward, King, the Third from the conquest   6.01
Named in the dating clause of the extent.

Eggerton, Philip de   6.07; **7.26**
Holder of 40 acres of land in Little Hollingworth, rendering 12d. + 12d. reveyeld and 4d. ward, and will do 'the same as above' ('haghehag', work of the mill and suit to the lord's mill). See *ChAcc2*, pp. 140–1.

Eton, Richard de   3.12; **6.62**; **7.12**; **7.14**; **7.22**
(Richard son of Robert de Eton **6.62**)
In **3.12** and **7.12** fifteen-year-old holder of half the manor of Hattersley by hereditary descent, knight service, reaping, ploughing, 'haghehag' and work of the mill. **3.13** and **7.14** add a share of 9d. for reveyeld and ward. In **6.62** and **7.22** holder

of the township of Werneth from the lord of Longdendale by knight service. Richard de Eton (alias Stokeport), only son of Robert de Eton (alias Stokeport) and Isabel Davenport (Earwaker, ii. 269, 274). In May 1354 it was found that the Black Prince had no right to the wardship of Richard son of **Robert de Eton**, since he held the manor of Stockport from Sir Hugh Despencer, and the manors of Poynton and Woodford from Geoffrey Poutrell. By 1369 both he and his two children had died: see the information from the Inquisition Post Mortem of Isabel de Stokeport his daughter and heiress (1370) provided in note 294, p. 71.

Eton, Robert de   **6.62**
Father of **Richard de Eton**, q.v.

Faber, Symon   **5.17**   See **Smith, Symon le**

Faber, Thomas   **4.40**   See **Smith, Thomas the**

Fernylegh, William del   **3.01**; **6.01**; **6.47**; **7.01**
(Possibly the person called William Symeson **4.51**.)
One of the jurors of **3.01**, **6.01** and **7.01**; joint holder at will (**6.47**) with others of Micklehurst and Littlehurst, for which they render 6½ marks (£4 6s. 8d.) a year. It is likely that William's share of the then rent for this property is represented in **4.51** where a Martinmas term payment of 10s. 11d. from William Symeson is recorded between the payments of two of the other co-tenants. The nearest Fern Lee appears to be at Greenfield, West Yorkshire, only a couple of miles N.E. of Micklehurst, but a Fernilee is situated in the Goyt Valley, S. of Whaley Bridge. In the 1408 Rental a Tho del Fernilegh paid 12s. 2¼d. as tenant at will in Micklehurst.

Forster, John son of Thomas le   **6.15**
Holder of one little house or building upon or above *le Syk*, presumably in Tintwistle, for 6d. a year.

Foucher (or **Foncher**), **Thomas le**   **4.21**; **6.60**
Holder at will (**6.60** with **4.21**) of Little Rudyng (presumably in Mottram) rendering 2s. a year. The name *Foucher* is found in Derbyshire (Sue Brown, Ranulf Higden Society, private communication). *O.E.D.* lists the verb 'fouch' as 'to divide a buck into four quarters'.

Fysse, [....] le   **1.35**

Fyton de Gous' (Gawsworth), **Thomas**   **2d1**
One of the Foresters of Macclesfield. Thomas Fyton was called 'Forester in Fee' in a land dispute in May 1354 (*B.P.R.,* iii. 160). He appears to have inherited the Orreby forestership (Earwaker, ii. 550–1). See *ChAcc2*, p. 146.

Gaunt (*or* **Gamit**), **Adam de**   **4.50**; **6.47**
Joint holder at will (**6.47**) with others of Micklehurst and Littlehurst, for which

they render 6½ marks (£4 6s. 8d.) a year. **4.50** appears to record his share of the Martinmas rent for this property at that date. In the Macclesfield Hundred Eyre Indictment Roll (CHES 25/20), m. 24, Adam de Ga(unt) de Sadilworthfrith and William son of William de Laylond were charged with the murder of Alexander son of Silvester de Oldome at Tintwistle on 4 June 1367. *Sadilworthfrith* (Saddleworth Forest) lay further up the Tame valley in Yorkshire.

Geffrou, William **3.01**; **4.48**; **5.24–25**; **6.01**; **6.08**; **6.19**; **7.01**
(Geffrou **3.01**, **6.01**, **6.19**, **7.01**, Geffreu **4.48**, **5.24**, **6.08**. N.B. In the Longdendale Account for 1359–60 (SC 6/802/17, m. 5) he is called 'son of Geoffrey'.)
One of the jurors of **3.01**, **6.01** and **7.01**, and also of **6.08**. In **6.19** with **4.48** he holds in fee one burgage with land adjacent (presumably in Tintwistle) for 2s., while in **5.24–25** two separate payments of 12d. are recorded, one for 1 acre, the other for *herstancloghous'*. Note that **6.21** records that *le Herstoncloghouses* with 6 acres of land adjacent used to render 4s., but is in decay. In the Longdendale accounts from 1357 to Lady Day 1361 the *Herstanclouhouses* of Tintwistle worth 4s. yearly were 'in decay' (the money could not be levied) because the lands were unploughed for lack of tenants. The **5.25** tenancy must therefore postdate Lady Day 1361. With others, William Geffrou farmed the agistment of Longdendale in 1359–60 and 1366–68 (SC 6/802/17, m. 5; 803/13, mm. 3 and 4).

Godard, Robert **4.37**
Mentioned by name only once, under Tintwistle, paying 6s. for Martinmas term. It seems likely that this Robert was here paying the rent due from *Ewodeheye*, **5.21**, *le Heewodeheyghe*, **6.42**. In the 1408 Rental a William Goddart paid 10s. ¼d. as a tenant at will in Tintwistle.

Godelegh (Godley)**, John de** **5.20**
In this entry 11s. 4d. is recorded under Tintwistle as received from the land of John de Godelegh. This appears to relate to the messuage with land adjacent held by **William son of John** in **6.55** and **William de Godelegh** in **4.14–15**. See also next entry.

Godelegh (Godley)**, William de** **4.14–15**; **6.55**
In **6.55**, among Mottram entries, **William son of John** holds 1 messuage with land adjacent at will and renders 9s. 6d. a year, of which reveyeld and ward 4d. This appears to be William de Godelegh, from whom Martinmas term receipts of 4s. 7d. + 2½d. for ward and revegeld are recorded in **4.14–15**. It appears from CCCIR 1373 that **Sir William Caryngton**, then farmer of the lordship of Longdendale, between the years 1361 and 1373 demolished *inter alia* a messuage in Mottram worth 20s. that was William de Godlye's, and during the same period gave him two oak trees.

Godelegh, [....] son of [....] de **1.10**

Godlegh (Godley)**, John son of John de** **3.11**; **7.11**
Holder of one messuage and 24 acres of land in Godley for 1d.

Godlegh (Godley), **Robert le Ward de**   **3.10**; **7.10**
Holder of half a carucate of land and one messuage in Godley, it is not known whether from the lord or others, but he does 'haghehag' & work of the mill.

Grene, [....] del   **1.30**

Gybon, Henry   **4.06–09**; **5.30**; **6.50**
In **6.50** with **4.06–07** and **5.30** holds at will in Mottram 1 messuage with land adjacent for 3s. + 4d. for ward and reveyeld. **4.08–09** records otherwise un-explained payments by him of 6½d. + 1½d. for parts of the land of **John de Hyde** (one messuage and 7 acres, and *Grenehouse*). See p. 23, notes 76f.

Gybonsone, William   **3.01**; **6.01**; [**7.01**]
(Gybonsone **3.01**, Gibonsone **6.01**)
Appears only as one of the jurors who gave evidence for the extent. Perhaps he appeared for, and was son of, **Henry Gybon**.

Haghe, Jordan del   **4.12–13**; **5.32**; **6.51**
(del Haghe **4.12–13**, **6.51**, del Hagh **5.32**)
Tenant at will (**6.51** with **4.12–13** and **5.32**) of 1 messuage with land adjacent in Mottram (presumably on 'the Hague') for 4s. 9d. + 4d. for reveyeld and ward.

Haghe, Wadkyn del   **4.19–20**   See **Ralph, Walter son of**

Halghton, Richard de   **4.38–39**; **5.04**; **6.38**
Tenant at will of *le Wallefeld* in Tintwistle for 9s. He may have taken his name from either Haughton Green, Lancashire, or Halton, Cheshire.

Harap, Adam de   **4.16**; **4.18**; **5.35**; **6.48**
(Harap **4.16**, **4.18**, **5.35**, Harop **6.48**)
Tenant at will of 1 messuage with land adjacent in Mottram (presumably in the vicinity of Harrop Edge) for 4s. 3d. a year. The joint payment with his brother **Stephen** of 7s. in **5.35** may indicate that they then held less land.

Harap, Stephen de, the elder   **4.02–03**; **5.29**; **6.52**
(Harap **4.02–03**, **5.29**, Harop **6.52**)
Tenant at will of 1 messuage, in **5.29** called *le Holehouse*, with land adjacent in Mottram for 4s. a year. In **4.03** he also paid 2d. at Martinmas term for land in *le Haghe*.

Harap, Stephen de, the younger   **4.17–18**; **5.35**; **6.49**
(Harap **4.17–18**, **5.35**, Harop **6.49**)
Tenant at will of 1 messuage with land adjacent in Mottram (presumably in the vicinity of Harrop Edge) for 4s. 3d. a year + 1d. The joint payment with his broth-er **Adam** of 7s. in **5.35** may indicate that they then held less land.

Hobrode, John   3.01; 4.33–34; 5.10; 6.01; 6.08; 6.34; 6.39; 6.40; 7.01
(Hobrode **3.01**, **4.33**, **6.01**, **6.08**, **6.34**, Hobrod **5.10**, Hobberode **6.39**, **7.01**)
One of the jurors of **3.01**, **6.01** and **7.01**, and also of **6.08**. In **6.34** with **4.34** and **5.10** he holds in fee 1 burgage with a certain toft in Tintwistle for 16d. a year. In **6.39**, he holds at will *le Wallecroft* (also in Tintwistle) for 3s. a year. In **6.40** with **Thomas le Barker** he holds at will a plot of land there rendering 10s. In **4.31** and **4.33** he and Thomas appear to be sharing equally the Martinmas rents of these two properties at 3s. 7d. each, but by the time of m. 5 they appear to have relinquished them. In the 1408 Rental the wife of Jo. de Hobrode paid 8¼d. as a free tenant and 3s. 1¾d. as a tenant at will in Tintwistle.

Holynworth (Hollingworth), **Christiana de**   4.70; 5.45; 6.06; 7.25
(Holynworth **4.70**, **5.45**, Holyn' **6.06**, **7.25**). It is not clear how this lady's first name would have been spoken in English, whether *Christine* or *Christiana*.)
Holder of two-thirds of the manor of Little Hollingworth by knight service, rendering for that and Thorntelegh (Thorncliffe) 3s. a year, 12d. for reveyeld, 4d. for ward, 'haghehag', work of the mill and suit to the lord's mill. In the 1408 Rental Tho de Holynwurth paid 1s. 6¼d. + 6¼d. for ward and reveyeld as a free tenant in Hollingworth, these payments not including *Thronkley*.

Holynworth, Henry son of Robert de   3.08; [4.68]; 7.06
Under-age holder of a quarter of the manor of Matley by knight service, by the service of 4s. for the whole manor (cf. **5.51**), by 'haghehag', by earthwork at Tintwistle mill whenever necessary, by performing suit at Mottram court and finding two doomsmen. The jury of 28 January 1360, which included his father, is not recorded as having mentioned that he was under age and thus a ward. The 1359–60 accounts (SC 6/802/17, m. 5) record for the first time the receipt of 6s. for the custody of the lands and tenements of Henry son and heir of Alice daughter of **William de Matley**, under age, viz. 14 that year, for a fourth part of the township of Matley. One such payment of 6s., by **John de Hyde**, is recorded in **4.68**. In **3.08** the most interesting service of 'haghehag' is defined.

Holynworth, John de   5.44; 6.04; 7.23
Holder by knight service of Great Hollingworth rendering 3s. 4d. a year, 'haghag', work of the mill, 7½d. a year for reveyeld, and 2½d. for ward, will find one doomsman and perform suit at Mottram court every three weeks. **7.23** states 2 doomsmen and adds suit to the lord's mill. In the 1408 Rental Jo de Holynwurth paid 1s. 9¾d. as free tenant in Hollingworth, + 4¼d. for ward and reveyeld. The absence from m. 4 of any appropriate entry for this manor is noteworthy but unexplained.

Holynworth, Robert de   3.01; 4.56–57; 6.01; 7.01
One of the jurors who gave evidence for the extent, **3.01**, **6.01**, **7.01**. His 14-year-old son **Henry** held a quarter of the manor of Matley. He may also have represented **John de Holynworth**. His Martinmas term payments in **4.56–57**, one of 6d., and another of 1d. for one plot of land next to the mill, are otherwise unexplained in these

manuscripts, though **4.56** may refer to *Oldefeld* (**6.07**, **7.26**, and **5.59**) and **4.57** to a plot next to the mill mentioned in **6.33** as held by **John son of William de Hyde**.

Holynworth, William son of Christiana de   **4.71**; **?4.72**
This William is not so named elsewhere in the manuscripts. It may be, however, that the William in question is otherwise known as **William de Thorntelegh**. His undefined payment of 1½d., perhaps together with the next entry of 4½d. from reveyeld, are not explained elsewhere in the manuscripts, though together they amount to a half-year's reveyeld due from **Christiana**.

Honford (Handforth), **Geoffrey de**   **3.09**; **3.14**; **7.09**; **7.15**
His four-year-old daughter and heiress (Katherine, unnamed in these manuscripts) holds by knight service (**3.09**, **7.09**) a quarter of the manor of Godley. She also shares with others (**3.14**, **7.15**) the holding by knight service of one messuage and one carucate of land in Mottram in *le Haghe*, rendering 4s. a year. The wardship and marriage of Geoffrey's daughter and heiress Katherine were on 13 Jan. 1361 granted to Robert de Legh the younger (*ChRR*, p. 288). In **Robert de Newton's** Inquisition Post Mortem of 1362 Geoffrey de Honford was called Lord of Godley, and his daughter and heiress Katherine, one of the people from whom the manor of Newton was held, was already wife of William son and heir of **William de Tranemol**, both under age and in the custody of the earl of Chester (Earwaker, ii. 161). **John le Tieu's** 1359–60 Account (SC 6/802/17, m. 5) reveals that the custody of the land of the heiress of Geoffrey de Honford had been leased to the township of Godley for 31s. 5½d. (including 17½d. of his own free rent) at Pentecost. It appears that Geoffrey's murder had been engineered by **John de Hyde, knight**, but actually carried out by Sir John's son William, Hugh Frenshie, and **John son of William de Hyde** in or before 1359–60. See *ChAcc2*, pp. 148–9.

Hune' or **Hund', William le**   **5.11**
This person whose name is not found in this form elsewhere in the manuscripts pays an annual rent of 16d. for a burgage or burgages in Tintwistle. For the reasons given in note 135 above *ad loc.* the possibility needs to be considered that he may have been more precisely identified either in **6.12–13** as **William Nyksone** or in **4.30** as **William son of Roger del Bothum**.

Hyde, John de (knight)   **3.06–07**; **3.09**; **3.11**; **3.14–15**; **3.18**; **4.08**; **4.66**; **?4.68**; **5.50**; **7.04–05**; **7.07**; **7.15–17**
Apparently unlawful holder of half the manor of Matley (which was held by knight service) (**3.06**, **7.04**); holder by knight service (**3.07**, **7.05**) of a quarter of the manor of Matley; holder by knight service (**3.09**, **7.07**) of half the manor of Godley, and renders a penny (**3.11**, **7.07**) for his tenement there; joint holder by knight service (**3.14**, **7.15**) of one messuage and one carucate of land in Mottram in *le Haghe* for 4s. a year; holder by knight service (**3.15**, **7.16** with **5.50**) of one messuage and seven acres of land at an unnamed place in Mottram for 13d. a year for which **Henry Gybon** paid in **4.08**; holder (**3.18**, **7.17**) of a place in Mottram

called *le Grenehouse/Grevehouse* for 3d. reveyeld + 1d. ward and makes suit to the mill. **4.66** and **4.68** record under Matley the Martinmas term receipts of 20d. from the land of John de Hyde, and 6s. from John de Hyde for the land in wardship of the son of **Robert de Holynworth** and it seems likely that Sir John is referred to in both. It appears that he was responsible for engineering the murder of **Geoffrey de Honford**, which was actually carried out by his son William, Hugh Frenshie and **John son of William de Hyde** in or before 1359–60. See Earwaker, ii. 157, and *ChAcc2*, pp. 148–9.

Hyde, John son of William de   **3.06**; **4.43**; **5.12**; [[**6.26b**]] **6.32–33**
Rightful holder by knight service (**3.06**) of half the manor of Matley, rendering 3d. reveyeld and 1d. ward. It is in this entry that the vernacular expression *drive & lede* is interlineated, expressing the obligation to perform suit of the lord's mill. In January 1360 this half of Matley was held by **John de Hyde**, **knight**, by what right the jurors did not know; but by the time of the 1359–60 account, i.e. Michaelmas 1360 (SC 6/802/17, m. 5) because of the rightful holder's having been outlawed for murder it had been taken into the lord's hand and leased at will to the tenants of the township at a rent of 40s. a year. (See below.) Holder in fee (**6.32** with **4.43** and **5.12**) of 6 burgages and 9 acres of land in Tintwistle for 14s. 5d. a year, and (**6.33**) a plot next to the mill which used to render 6d. a year. In **5.12** the marginal note *levab'* may be future tense 'will be levied', but the imperfect 'used to be levied' is also possible, and again presumably reflects his having been outlawed. The deleted entry at **6.26b** stated that he formerly held *le Smolterhouses* for 12d. John son of William de Hyde forfeited half the township of Matley because of his participation in the death of **Geoffrey de Honford** and by 1366 the lands, valued at £2 10s., were leased to Margaret Hulm (SC 6/803/13, m. 3).

Hyde, William de   **3.06**, [**7.04**]
Deceased holder by knight service of half the manor of Matley. This right descended first to his son Richard, then on his decease to Richard's brother John, but at the time of the making of the extent the land was in the possession of **John de Hyde, knight**, by what right the jurors did not know. This statement may help to explain why by Pentecost (24 May) 1360 this half of Matley had been taken into the hands of the lord of Longdendale. See previous entry and Earwaker, ii. 157. It appears from CCCIR 1373 that **Sir William Caryngton**, then farmer of the lordship of Longdendale, between 1361 and 1373 demolished *inter alia* a hall and chamber in Tintwistle worth £10 that were William de Hyde's.

Hyrnet, [....]   **1.26**

John, William son of   **6.55**   See above, **Godelegh, William de**

Lastles, John   **3.01**; **6.01**; **6.47**; [**7.01**]
One of the jurors who gave evidence for the extent (**3.01**, **6.01**, [**7.01**]) and joint holder at will with others (**6.47**) of Micklehurst and Littlehurst, for which they

render 6½ marks a year (£4 6s. 8d.). He may have been connected with the Astle or Asthulle family of Chelford or Wilmslow. It is significant that he is not one of the tenants named in m. 4.

Mattelegh (Matley), **William de   4.67**
This entry records under Matley a payment of 2s. 4d. from his land, which presumably relates to the share of the 4s. annual free rent of Matley due from the half held by the now outlawed **John son of William de Hyde**.

Maykin, Richard son of Thomas   1.15

Merser, Robert le   6.36
Former tenant of a certain burgage now lying in decay which used to render 12d. a year. This burgage was recorded under 'Decay of Rent' in the Longdendale accounts throughout the period 1358–61 (SC 6/802/15, m. 1, m. 1d; 802/17, m. 5; 803/3, m. 5).

Muleward, Simon le   4.54; 6.47
(*molendinario* **4.54**, le Muleward **6.47**)
Joint holder at will with others of Micklehurst and Littlehurst, for which they render 6½ marks a year (£4 6s. 8d.). His presence in this partnership presumably implies the existence of a mill in the valley of the Tame or one of its tributaries, perhaps in the Micklehurst area or at Millbrook.

Mulner, William le   1.09; 4.27; 5.23; 6.44
Holder at will of 2 messuages with land adjacent in Tintwistle for 11s. a year. He seems to have operated the mill at Tintwistle, with gaps, until Michaelmas 1367. See Tables, pp. xxxviiiff.

Neuton (Newton), **Robert de   3.01; 3.05; 6.01; 7.03**
One of the jurors who gave evidence for the extent (**3.01, 6.01**, presumably in the lacuna in **7.01**) and holder by knight service and other services (**3.05, 7.03**) of the manor of Newton. The other services of reaping and ploughing, with their conditions there described, reflect the formal survival of ancient patterns of tenure, though it should be noted that **5.54** and the Longdendale accounts record the annual receipt of 11s. 1d. in lieu. His Inquisition Post Mortem of 1362 (Earwaker, ii. 161) reveals that he held the manor of Newton in Longdendale of **John de Hyde, knight, Howel ap Owein Voyl**, William son and heir of **William de Tranemel** and Katharine daughter and heiress of **Geoffrey de Honford** by knight's service, viz. the 32nd part of one knight's fee. In the 1408 Rental the plough-services (*arrures*) of Newton produced 8s. 1d.

Nyksone, William   6.12–13
Named only here as the holder (presumably in Tintwistle) of one grange and one curtilage rendering 4d. a year, and of one toft rendering 2d. a year. See also **William le Hune** or **Hund** above.

Olde, [....]   **1.18**

Oweyn Voyl, Howel ap   **3.09**; **3.14**; **7.08**; **7.15**
Joint holder with the heir of **William de Tranemol** by knight service (**3.09**, **7.08**) of one quarter of the manor of Godley, and joint holder with **John de Hyde (knight)**, the heir of **William de Tranemol** and the daughter and heiress of **Geoffrey de Honford** by knight service (**3.14**, **7.15**) of one messuage and one carucate of land in Mottram in *le Haghe* rendering 4s. a year. Howel ap Oweyn Voel was kinsman and heir of William Boydell in 1354 (*D.K.R. 36* (1875), Appendix II, p. 136).

Padfield, Robert de   **1.01**

Prestessone, Thomas le   **4.52**; **6.47**
(son of Richard the chaplain **4.52**, le Prestessone **6.47***)*
Joint holder at will with others of Micklehurst and Littlehurst, for which they render 6½ marks a year (£4 6s. 8d.). **4.52** records the Martinmas term payment of his portion of the rent for this property at that time.

Radeclyft (Radcliffe), **John son of John de**   **6.02**; **7.20**
(Radeclyft **6.02**, Radeclyf' **7.20**)
Holder by unspecified service of one messuage with a garden and half a rood of land in Mottram for 1¼d. a year. **7.20** adds that he makes suit to the lord's mill. In July 1364 John son of John de Radeclif successfully obtained the lands of his wife Margaret, which had been in the Black Prince's hands during her minority. She was heiress of Isabel, widow of Sir Thomas Danyers. *B.P.R.*, iii. 470.

Ralph, Walter son of   **5.33**
Rowessone, Watkyn   **6.53**
Haghe, Wadkyn del   **4.19–20**
These references are almost certainly to the same person, holder at will of 1 messuage with land adjacent (presumably on 'the Hague' in Mottram) for which he renders (**6.53**, with **4.19–20**) 6s. 3d. a year + 4d. for ward and reveyeld. The 7s. in **5.53** may imply that he then occupied more land. Rowe is taken to be another form of Ralph: Old Roe's tomb in Mottram Church has traditionally been considered to be that of Sir Ralph de Stavelegh, and Watkyn is a diminutive of Walter (Earwaker, ii. 119).

Richard (the chaplain), Thomas son of   **4.52** See above, **Prestessone, Thomas le**

Richard, [....] son of   **1.27**

Riggeway, Richard de   **4.04–05**; **5.34**
(Riggeway **4.04**, Ruggeway **5.34**)
Recorded in these entries as paying the Martinmas term and annual rents from the property held in **6.58–59** by **Hugh del Ruggeway**, see below. It appears from

CCCIR 1373 that **Sir William Caryngton**, then farmer of the lordship of Longdendale, between the years 1361 and 1373 demolished *inter alia* a messuage in Mottram worth 20s. that was Richard de Riggesway's.

Roger, Robert son of Symon son of   1.03

Rowessone, Watkyn   **6.53** See above, **Ralph, Walter son of**

Ruggeway, Hugh del   **6.58–59**
Holder at will of 1 messuage with land adjacent (presumably in Mottram) for which he renders 14s. a year and 3¼d. for ward and reveyeld. It appears that **Richard de Riggeway** (see above) made these payments in membranes 4 and 5.

Smith, Symon le   **5.17; 6.31**
(*Symonis fabri* **5.17**, Symon le Smith **6.31**)
Entry **6.31** describes this former tenant's plot with curtilage as lying in decay but formerly rendering 9d. a year, while **5.17** records the annual receipt of 7d. from it. In the Longdendale accounts this burgage was listed under 'Decay of Rent' from Michaelmas 1359 to Lady Day 1361 (SC 6/802/17, m. 5, 803/3, m. 5) indicating that **5.17** must be later.

Smith, Thomas the   **4.40**
(*de Thoma Fabro*)
This entry recording a Martinmas term rent of 3d. appears to relate to the property listed in the next entry.

Smyth, Henry le (of Stokport)   **6.28**
Holder in fee of one messuage with a certain forge (presumably in Tintwistle) for which he renders 6d. a year. This may be the property for which the Martinmas term receipt of 3d. from **Thomas the Smith** is recorded in **4.40**.

Smyth, Robert le   **5.15**
This entry records an annual payment of 12d. for a burgage in Tintwistle. This Robert is referred to only here in these manuscripts, and the burgage has not been otherwise identified, though **6.36–37** refer to burgages 'in decay' with rents of 12d., and the latter which had been 'in decay' from 1357 ceased to be so in the 1359–60 account, presumably being occupied after the extent had been made in January of that year (SC 6/802/17, m. 5). A certain Robert le Smyth of Stayley took the mill of Tintwistle at farm for a term of six years at a rent of 15s. a year from Michaelmas 1367 (SC 6/803/13, m. 4).

Smyth, Robert le (the elder)   **5.16, 6.30**
Former tenant of a burgage described (**6.30**) as one messuage upon or above *le Syk*, which renders 7d. a year and was evidently occupied both in **6.30** and in **5.16**.

Smyth, [....] le   **1.06**

Spener, Thomas le   1.14

Stanlegh, Richard de   2d5
One of the Foresters of Macclesfield, who took his name from Distley Stanley. Called Forester of Macclesfield c. 1357 (*B.P.R.*, iii. 253). He farmed the coalmines within the forest for 8s. in 1360–61 (SC 6/803/3, m. 4). See also Earwaker, ii. 88–9.

Staveley (Stayley), **Robert de**   **3.01**; **3.04**; **6.01**; **7.01**; **7.27**
(Staveley **3.01**, **6.01**, **7.01**, Stavelegh **3.04**, **7.27** heading)
One of the jurors who gave evidence for the extent. **3.04** and **7.27** explain that he holds the manor of Stayley from the lord of Longdendale by knight service, but that he also has a day (is given notice) to show by what other services he holds the same manor. From **2.04** and the 1359–60 accounts it is clear that these services (like others) were commuted for cash payment. In the 'Respites' section of the 1359–60 accounts (SC 6/802/17, m. 5) he was granted respite of rents, works and services for the previous 18 months (13s. 1d. + 6s. 6½d.) because he had shown a relaxation by the previous lord, Robert de Holand.

Stiwardesson, William le   6.37
Former holder of 1 burgage now lying in decay which used to render 12d. a year. Since this property was listed in decay in the account of the escheator who took over the management of the lordship and his successors for the period Michaelmas 1357–Michaelmas 1359, this is likely to have been the son of Robert de Holand's steward (SC 6/802/15, m 1.)

Sutton, John de   2d2
One of the Foresters of Macclesfield. John de Sutton was succeeded as Forester of Macclesfield by his kinsman John son of Richard de Sutton in 1362 (*B.P.R.*, iii. 450–1). See next below.

Sutton, John son of Richard de   2d4
One of the Foresters of Macclesfield. The Suttons appear to have held two forester-ships, one for lands in Disley, the other for lands in Sutton; the former held 'as of ancient tenure, in fee and inheritance', the latter held 'by deed of Earl Hugh'. There are two Suttons also in Earwaker's list of Macclesfield foresters, which he believes to date from about the end of the thirteenth century (Earwaker, ii. 6–7, 90, 439).

Symeson, William   4.51
This is probably the patronymic of **Fernylegh, William del**, q. v.

Symon son of Roger, Robert son of   1.03

Tayllour, Adam le   5.36
This entry is among the annual payments from Mottram: 'From Adam le Tayllour 10s. 1d. in decay.' It is altogether unclear to which Mottram lands this entry may

relate, and this Adam is not so named elsewhere in these mss. See note 158 *ad loc.*, pp. 37–9, and Introduction, p. xx.

Tern[..], Henry le   **1.04**

Thorntelegh (Thorncliffe), **William de**   **3.01**; **4.45**; **5.18**; **6.01**; **6.08**; **6.41**; [**7.01**]
(Throntel' **3.01**, Thorntelegh **4.45**, **5.18**, **6.08**, Throntelegh **6.01**, Thornley **6.41**, [.....]elegh **7.01**).
There was evidently considerable variation locally in the pronunciation and hence spelling of this name, exemplifying the process, not uncommon in Old and Middle English, known as 'metathesis of post-vocalic r' (Mrs Anne Read, formerly of Leeds University, private communication.) Note that in **3.01** the scribe had first written *Thornclyf*, which sounds like the modern name, but then presumably at the insistence of William, or the jury in general, corrected it to *Throntel'*, presumably intended as a suspended form of *Throntelegh*. The 1408 Rental has *Thronkley*, and R. Bretland's accompanying letter of 1665, MS. Harl. 2039, f. 114, mentions old deeds (date unspecified but lost during the Civil War) with the spellings *Hornkley* and *Hornecley*. Cf. Earwaker, ii. 146, n. 1.
   One of the jurors who gave evidence for the extent (**3.01**, **6.01**, [**7.01**]), and also for the Inquisition of **6.08**. Holder at will (**6.41** with **4.45** and **5.18**) of 1 burgage with lands adjacent (presumably in Tintwistle) rendering 14s. 6d. a year. This William may also be referred to (**4.71**) as **William son of Christiana de Holynworth**.

Tieu, John le   **6.11**; **6.43**
Holder (**6.11**) of one burgage rendering 10d. a year, and holder at will (**6.43**) of one meadow (presumably in Tintwistle) for 14d. a year. John le Tieu (also spelled Tuwe), described as 'the Prince's servant', acted as deputy to Sir John Chandos from 3 April 1359 to Lady Day 1361 when **Sir William Caryngton** was granted his first lease, and in doing so rendered account for the lordship of Longdendale throughout that period (SC 6/802/15, m. 1d and 803/3, m. 4d). See *ChAcc2*, p. 181, Introduction, p. xii and Table 1, p. xxxviii.

Tillessone, Ralph   **4.58–59**; **6.56**
(Tillessone **4.58**, Tyllessone **6.56**)
Holder at will (**6.56** with **4.59**) of (Thomerode) rendering 2s. a year. This (probably incompletely deciphered) place-name does not appear elsewhere in these mss, and has not so far been identified. It appears, however, among what seem to be Mottram entries. In **4.58** he is recorded as paying a Martinmas rent of 18d. for unspecified land in Mottram, which seems likely to be for the land described in **3.17** and **7.19** as a messuage and eight acres held by **Ralph de Wolegh**, and named in **5.48** as *Brodlathum*. The possibility therefore needs to be considered that Tillesone may have been Ralph de Wolegh's patronymic.

Tranemol, William de   **3.09**; **3.14**; **7.08**; **7.15**
(Tranemol **3.09**, **3.14**, Tranemell **7.08**, Tranemoll **7.15**)
His son and heir holds jointly with **Howel ap Oweyn** (**3.09**, **7.08**) a quarter of the township of Godley by knight service. The same heir holds jointly with **Sir John de Hyde**, **Howel ap Oweyn**, and the heiress of **Geoffrey de Honford** by knight service (**3.14**, **7.15**) one messuage and one carucate of land in Mottram in *le Haghe*. By 1362 his son William was already married to Katharine, daughter of **Geoffrey de Honford** (IPM of Robert de Newton).

Tyllessone, Ralph   **6.56** See **Tillessone, Ralph** above

Upton, Edmund de   **2d7**
One of the Foresters of Macclesfield. An Edmund de Upton farmed the lands in Marple of Richard Vernon who was a ward in 1351 (SC 6/802/7, m. 1). He appears to have taken over temporarily the Vernon forestership. See also Earwaker, ii. 50.

Wade, [....] son of William   **1.02**

Warde, John le   **1.11**

Wharell, William del   **4.22–23**; **5.31**; **6.54**
Holder at will (**6.54** with **4.22–23**) of one messuage with land adjacent in Mottram rendering 2s. 10d. a year + 2½d. for ward and revegeld. **5.31** however records under Mottram an annual receipt from him of 7s., possibly for more land. Wharell is taken to be Warhill, the hill on which Mottram Church stands (Dodgson, i. 315) and the nearby farm. See Nevell & Walker, p. 74, Plate 5.1.

William, Nicholas son of   **5.06**; [[**6.21b**]]; **6.25**
(N. son of William son of Thomas **6.25**, **6.21b** adds Dykeson)
Holder in fee (**6.25** with **5.06**) of 2 burgages and 3 tofts with appurtenances (one croft) in Tintwistle rendering 3s. 10d. a year. The deleted entry **6.21b** mentioned 'a parcel of land there of Nicholas son of William son of Thomas Dykeson' rendering 2d. a year.

William, [....] son of   **1.23**,   and **John his son**   **1.24**

Wolegh, (Woolley) **Ralph de**   **3.01**; **3.17**; **5.48**; **7.19**
From the cross by his name in **3.01** it appears that although Ralph de Wolegh was summoned to appear on the jury which gave evidence for the extent he did not attend. Holder 'by the same services' (**3.17**, **7.19** with **5.48**) of 1 messuage and eight acres of land in Mottram rendering 3s. a year. The contexts in m. 3 and m. 7 leave it unclear precisely what these services were, except that they did not include suit of the mill, though the 1359–60 accounts indicate that haghehag was included. See above, pp. xxvif. From **5.48** where he is listed among the free

tenants in Longdendale it is clear that this property was called *le Brodlathum*, and the appropriate Martinmas rent was in **4.58** paid by **Ralph Tillessone**, raising the possibility that that was his patronymic. Woolley is a hamlet in Hollingworth township on the borders of Cheshire and Derbyshire. In 1349 Ralph de Woley (nephew of Richard) became possessed of lands in Broadbottom, as above, and these lands remained in the family until the sixteenth century at least (Earwaker, ii. 154; H.T.Milliken, *Saga of a Family* (London, 1967), pp. 2–3).

Wolegh, Richard de   **1.12**; **3.01**; **4.61–62**; **5.46**; **6.01**; **6.05**
One of the jurors who gave evidence for the extent (**3.01**, **6.01**) and holder (**6.05** with **4.61–62** and **5.46**) of a third part of Little Hollingworth, finding one dooms-man, making suit to the Court of Mottram and giving 12d. a year + 1½d. for reveyeld and ½d. for ward. See **Ralph de Wolegh**, above.

Worth, Thomas de   **2d6**
One of the Foresters of Macclesfield. About 1362 a certain William de Hulme obtained the forestership of Thomas de Worth from the earl of Chester (Earwaker, ii. 341). See *ChAcc2*, p. 190.

Wylde, Henry le   **4.35–36**; **5.03**; **5.08**; **6.27**; **6.29**
Holder in fee for the term of his wife's life (**6.27** with **4.35** and, inconsistently, **5.08**) of 1 burgage with one toft rendering 21d. a year. Holder at will (**6.29** with **4.37** and **5.03**) of one burgage with *le Rodefeld* rendering 8s. 6d. a year. Dodgson, i. 325 suggests that this may be identified with Rhodeswood. In the 1408 Rental Adam le Wylde paid separate rents of 2¼d. and 1¼d. as a free tenant, and 3s. 6¼d. for *le Blake-erth* as a tenant at will in Tintwistle.

[.......], John   **1.08**

[...]ller, [.... ...] of Adam   **1.13**

BIBLIOGRAPHY

MANUSCRIPTS AND PRINTED WORKS CITED

Manuscript sources

The following manuscripts are preserved in the Department of Manuscripts at the British Library.

MS. Harl. 2039, f. 113: Rental of Longdendale 9 Henry 4, cited as 1408 Rental, and f. 114: the associated letter from Reginald Bretland of Thorncliffe to Randle Holme of Chester dated 11 April 1665.

MS. Harl. 6353, 7, ff. 121–50: a copy of Sir Henry Spelman's *Archaismus Graphicus* (1606).

The following manuscripts are preserved in the Public Record Office, now incorporated into The National Archives at Kew.

CHES 3/6 (28): Inquisition Post Mortem of Isabel Stockport, 1370.

CHES 25/4 County Court of Chester Indictments Roll (1354–77), m. 29, in a transcript kindly provided by the late Mrs Phyllis Hill of the Ranulf Higden Society, referred to as CCCIR 1373.

CHES 25/20 Macclesfield Hundred Eyre Indictments Roll. (Noted by Paul Booth.)

SC 6/786/7, m. 4: Accounts of divers ministers, Chester & Cheshire, 1366–67, noted by Paul Booth.

SC 6/786/10, m. 4: Accounts of divers ministers, Chester & Cheshire, 1368–69, noted by Paul Booth.

SC 6/802/1, r. 2: Macclesfield Ministers' Accounts, 1329–30, cited in *D.M.L.*, s.v. *becagium*.

SC 6/802/6: Macclesfield Steward's Account, 1350–51, cited in *D.M.L.*, s.v. *becagium*.

SC 6/802/7: Macclesfield Ministers' Accounts, 1351, noted by Paul Booth: m. 1 also cited in *D.M.L.*, s.v. *becagium*.

SC 6/802/11, m. 2: Macclesfield Ministers' Accounts, 1354–55, noted by Paul Booth.

SC 6/802/15, m. 1: Account of Henry de Prestbury, deputy bailiff of Longdendale, 13 September 1358–3 April 1359; and Account of Thomas le Yonge, escheator of Cheshire, for the issues of the lands and tenements which had been Robert de Holand's in Longdendale, Michaelmas 1357–13 September 1358.

SC 6/802/15, m. 1d: Account of John le Tieu, deputy steward and bailiff of the lordship of Longdendale, 3 April 1359–Michaelmas 1359.

SC 6/802/17, m. 5 and 6/803/1, m. 6: Account of John le Tieu, deputy steward of the lordship of Longdendale, Michaelmas 1359–Michaelmas 1360.

SC 6/802/17, m. 5d: Account of Richard Vernon, Edmund de Downes, Thomas Fyton, John de Sutton, Thomas Worth, Richard de Stanlegh, John de Pycton and Roger Dyken, foresters of Macclesfield Forest and collectors of Macclesfield Forest Eyre fines, 1359–60 and 1361–62; and Account of Thomas le Yonge, escheator of

101

Cheshire, for the issues of the lands and tenements which had been Robert de Holand's in Longdendale, Michaelmas 1357–13 September 1358 (another copy).

SC 6/803/1, m. 6: Another, better, copy of 6/802/17, m. 5d. See above.

SC 6/803/3, m. 5: Account of John le Tieu, deputy steward and bailiff of the lordship of Longdendale for the issues of the same lordship, Michaelmas 1360–26 March 1361; and Account of William de Carinton, knight, farmer of the lordship of Longdendale, Lady Day–Michaelmas 1361.

SC 6/803/4: Another copy of 6/803/3.

SC 6/803/5, m. 1–m. 2: Account of Macclesfield Forest Bailiff and Account of William de Caryngton, knight, farmer of the lordship of Longdendale, 1361–62. Now published in Booth, *Maccl. Acc.*, pp. 10f., 24–31. See below.

SC 6/803/12, m. 3: Account of William de Carynton, knight, farmer of the lordship of Longdendale, Michaelmas 1365–Lady Day 1366; and (m. 3–m. 3d) View of the account of Adam de Kyngeslegh, bailiff of Longdendale, Lady Day–30 September 1366.

SC 6/803/13, m. 3: Account of Adam de Kyngeslegh, bailiff of the lordship of Longdendale, Lady Day 1366–26 March 1367.

SC 6/803/13, m. 4: Account of John de Scolehalgh, steward of the lordship of Longdendale, Lady Day 1367–Lady Day 1368.

SC 6/803/15, m. 2d: Account of William Caryngton, knight, of the issues of the lordship there, Lady Day–11 April 1368, and Account of the same William, of the issues of the aforesaid lordship, 11 April 1368–30 September 1368.

SC 6/804/7, m. 3d: Account of William de Caryngton, knight, farmer there, Michaelmas 1374–28 November next following.

SC 11/897, mm. 1–7: 'Extent of the lordship of Longdendale 34 Edward III' (later title).

Printed books

Aikin, John, *A Description of the Country from Thirty to Forty Miles Round Manchester* (Manchester, 1795), cited as Aikin.

Baines, Edward, *History of the County Palatine of Lancaster* (London, 1831).

Booth, P.H.W. and Carr, A.D., eds., *Account of Master John de Burnham the Younger, Chamberlain of Chester, of the Revenues of the Counties of Chester and Flint, 1361–62*, R.S.L.C., cxxv (1991), cited as *ChAcc2*.

Booth, P.H.W., ed., *Accounts of the Manor and Hundred of Macclesfield, Cheshire, Michaelmas 1361 to Michaelmas 1362*, R.S.L.C., cxxxviii (2003), cited as *Maccl. Acc.*

Dawes, M.C.B., *Register of Edward the Black Prince*, 4 vols (London, 1930–33), cited as *B.P.R.*

Dodgson, J.McN., *The Place-Names of Cheshire*, 4 vols (Cambridge, 1970), cited as Dodgson.

Earwaker, J.P., *East Cheshire Past and Present*, 2 vols (London, 1880), cited as Earwaker.

Hartley, Marie and Ingilby, Joan, *Life & Tradition in the Yorkshire Dales* (London, 1968).

Latham, R.E. et al., eds., *Dictionary of Medieval Latin from British Sources* (London, O.U.P. for the British Academy, 1975– [in progress]), cited as *D.M.L.*

Maddicott, J.R., *Thomas of Lancaster 1307–22: a Study in the Reign of Edward II* (London, O.U.P., 1970).

Milliken, H.T., *Saga of a Family, the Story Behind the House of Woolley* (London, British Drug Houses Ltd., 1967).

Myers, A. R., *England in the Late Middle Ages*, 8th edition (Harmondsworth, 1971).

Nevell, Michael and Walker, John, *Lands and Lordships in Tameside* (Tameside, 1998), cited as Nevell & Walker.

P.R.O. *Calendar of the Patent Rolls Preserved in the Public Record Office ... Edward III, A.D. 1327–[1377]* (London, HMSO, 1891–1916), cited as *C.P.R.*

P.R.O. *Calendar of Recognizance Rolls of the Palatinate of Chester* in *36th Annual Report of the Deputy Keeper of the Public Records* (1875), cited as *ChRR*.

P.R.O. *Report of the Deputy Keeper of the Public Records*, 36 (London, HMSO, 1875), cited as *D.K.R.*

Simpson, J.A. & Weiner, E.S.C., eds, *Oxford English Dictionary*, 2nd edn (Oxford, 1989), cited as *O.E.D.*

Steinberg, S.H., *Five Hundred Years of Printing*, new edn revised by John Trevitt (London, the British Library, 1996).

Stewart-Brown, R., ed., *Calendar of County Court, City Court and Eyre Rolls of Chester, 1257–1297, with an Inquest of Military Service, 1288*, Chetham Society, New Series, 84 (1925).

INDEX OF PERSONS

*Figures in bold (**1.17**) indicate entries in the record, other figures show page numbers.*

104

INDEX OF PLACES

Figures in bold (**3.05**) *indicate entries in the record, other figures show page numbers*

Lancaster, County Palatine of xviii, 102
Littlehurst xf., xvi, xix, xxi, xxviii, xxxf., xlf.,
  xliiiff., 15, 27, 29, **5.38**, **6.47**, 80, 85, 88,
  93ff.
Little Rudyng 25, **6.60**, 76, 88
Liverpool 51
London 102f.
Longdendale ix–xvi, xviii–xxiii, xxvif., xxix,
  xxxi, xxxiiif., xxxviii, xl, xliiiff., xlixf., **m.
  1d**, 6–9, **2.10**, 13, **3.04**, **3.11**, **5.01**, 35, 37,
  5.39, **5.43**, 41, **5.65**, **6.01**, **6.62–64**, **7.04**,
  7.10, **7.22**, **7.27**, 71f., 81, 83ff., 88f., 93f.,
  96–102

Macclesfield vii, xi, xv, xxiii, xxvi, xxxi, xxxiv,
  xxxvii, xliv, 7, 10f., 17, 27, 45, 61, 85, 87f.,
  97, 99–102

Manchester ix, xxxvii, 102
Marple 11, 99
Matley x, xvf., xix, xxif., xxiv–xxvii, xxixf.,
  xxxviii–xlii, xlivf., li, **2.05**, 13, **3.06–08**,
  4.64–65, 31, **5.51**, **5.63**, **7.04–06**, 73,
  91–94
Mediterranean Sea xxvi, 47
Mersey xlf., xlv, 85
Micklehurst xf., xvi, xix, xxi, xxviii, xxxf., xlf.,
  xliiiff., 15, 27, 29, **5.38**, **6.47**, 80, 88,
  93ff.
Millbrook 94
Mossley 57
Mottram x, xvff., xx–xxiii, xxv, xxvii–xxxi,
  xxxviii–xlv, xlixf., **2.02**, 9, 13, 17, 19, **3.08**,
  3.13–18, **4.01–25**, 29, 35, **5.28–37**, 39, 41,
  5.50, 43, **6.02–05**, 49, **6.48–60**, **7.06**, **7.13**,
  7.15–21, **7.23**, 74ff., 81, 83–86, 88–92,
  95–100

Newton x, xv, xxif., xxivff., xxviii, xxxi,
  xxxviii–xli, xlviii, **2.03**, 13, **3.05**, 19, **5.54**,
  7.03, 73, 92, 94
Northenden 41, 83

Oldefeld 29, **5.59**, 49, 77, 82, 92
Oxford 103

Padfield **1.01**

Poynton 21, 88
Prestefeld xlif., 39

Radcliffe 47, 95
Rhodeswood 25, 100
Riddings 59: see also Little Rudyng.
Rodefeld **4.36**, **5.03**, **6.29**, 79, 100
Roe Cross xlix, 59
Rontandebrok xxvii, **6.65**, 83

Saddleworth 27, 89
Sadilworthfrith 27, 89
Sale 19, 85
Salter's Brook ix, xxvii, lii, **6.65**, 83
Sheffield ix
Smolterhouses, le xxviiif., xxxiii, **6.26b**, 87, 93
Snake Pass ix
Staffordshire 17
Stayley x, xv, xx–xxiii, xxvf., xxxf.,
  xxxviii–xliii, xlv, xlvii, **2.04**, 13, **3.04**, 35,
  5.53, **5.63**, 67, **7.27**, 72, 96f.
Stockport xx, 21, 27, 88
Sutton 11
Syk, le xxix, 35, **6.15**, **6.30**, 77, 79, 88, 96

Tameside xxii, xxxvii, 15, 39, 103
Tame valley x, xvif., xxi, xxviii, 15, 27, 39, 89, 94
(Thomerode) 29, **6.56**, 76, 98
Thorncliffe x, xvi, xxi, xxiv, 13, 31, 39, 43, 47,
  6.06, 49, **7.25**, 77, 91, 98, 101
Tintwistle ix–xii, xvif., xxf., xxivf., xxvii–xxxi,
  xxxiii, xxxviii–xlv, xlixff., **2.01**, 9, 13, 15,
  17, **3.08**, **4.26–54**, 31, **5.02–27**, 39, **6.08–44**,
  57, **7.06**, 71, 75, 77–80, 82–94, 96, 98ff.
Tranmere 19

Wallecroft, le xxi, 15, **6.39**, 79, 91
Wallefeld, le 27, **5.04**, **6.38**, 79, 90
Warhill 25, 99
Werneth x, xvi, xxii, **6.62**, **7.22**, 80, 88
Whaley Bridge 15, 88
Wilmslow 15, 94
Woodford 21, 88
Woodhead ix
Woolley xlif., xlix, 13, 29, 85, 100

Yorkshire ix, lii, 15, 17, 27, 61, 88f., 102

SUBJECT INDEX

*Figures in bold (**3.11**) indicate entries in the record, other figures show page numbers*

110